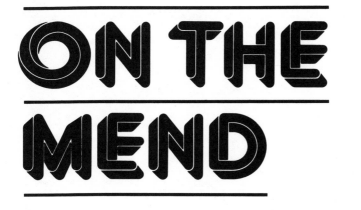

ON THE MEND

GETTING AWAY FROM DRUGS

By Maxine B. Rosenberg

Bradbury Press · New York

Maxwell Macmillan Canada · Toronto
Maxwell Macmillan International
New York · Oxford · Singapore · Sydney

To Barry Fenstermacher,
who believes in children

All the photographs in this book were taken by Maxine B. Rosenberg except for
the photographs on pages 56–58, which were supplied by the New York State
Division of Substance Abuse Services, Marcia Oliveri, photographer and the
photograph on page 55, which was supplied by Smith/Greenland, Inc.

Library of Congress Cataloging-in-Publication Data   Rosenberg, Maxine
B.   On the mend : getting away from drugs / by Maxine B. Rosenberg.   p.   cm.   Includes bibliographical references and
index.   Summary: Eight young people talk about their experiences with
drugs: how and why they started, factors influencing their decisions to stop, and
their recovery from addiction.   ISBN 0-02-777914-9   1. Drug abuse—
United States—Case studies—Juvenile literature.   2. Youth—United
States—Drug use—Case studies—Juvenile literature.   3. Narcotic addicts—
Rehabilitation—United States—Case studies—Juvenile literature. [1. Drug
abuse.] I. Title.   HV5809.5.R67 1991
     362.29′0835—dc20   91-11202

ACKNOWLEDGMENTS

My grateful thanks to the following people and organizations who have made this book possible: Janet Eldon of the Week-end Center, Mt. Kisco, New York, for her belief and trust in the project; Doreen Lockwood of Daytop Village, Inc., Hartsdale, New York, for her invaluable time and support; the staff of Daytop Village, Inc., in the Bronx, New York; Catherine M. Quimby, Harry Rockland-Miller, and Jennifer Di Benedetto of Four Winds Hospital, Katonah, New York, for their time, concern, and interest in the book; Marcia Oliveri of the New York State Division of Substance Abuse Services for supplying a number of the photographs; Diane Maroney for leading me to the right source; my editor, Sharon Steinhoff, for her steadfast belief in the project; my daughter, Karin, who's helped me see things from a teenager's point of view; my husband, Paul, for being the wonderful person he is; and most of all, the eight young people in this book who have trusted me with the details of their lives so others can be helped.

Other Books by Maxine B. Rosenberg

Not My Family
Growing Up Adopted
Talking About Stepfamilies

CONTENTS

AUTHOR'S NOTE

WHEN I WAS first asked to write a book about young people and drugs, I was hesitant. Though I've tackled difficult family issues—alcoholism, adoption, and stepfamilies—in my other books, I feared that interviewing for this new project would feel like endless tales of kids trying hard to destroy their lives. After more thought, however, I realized the book could also be the story of how young people worked hard to change despite tremendous obstacles—a theme that interests me enormously. How could I not say yes?

Although the facts and statistics of drugs are astonishing—a recent study indicated that nearly one in three teenagers admitted to illicit drug use—my intention was to focus on the why. Why did young people turn to drugs and, then, what motivated some to seek treatment? Amazingly, I found little information on this subject from books and articles available in the library. More helpful were the professionals I spoke to who worked with young addicts in recovery. Also illuminating was sitting in at a team meeting at a hospital treatment center, which gave me a multifaceted view of the problems that accompany rehabilitation.

When I was ready to begin interviewing, I had no trouble finding young people who wanted to share their stories. Six volunteered after their counselor at their treatment center told them about the project. Two other interviewees were friends of people I knew. Each initial interview lasted two and a half hours or longer, with many back and forth phone calls over the next nine months. Those who agreed to be photographed met with me again. By the time the book was completed, I had a close relationship with each individual.

Of the eight young people interviewed, five grew up in suburban homes. One or both of their parents worked, while the children attended schools where the majority of students went on to college. Even the young man who lived in a poorer city neighborhood came from a family that was able to afford private-school education for him. In fact, to outsiders, all but one of the families appeared "normal." Yet within the homes there were signs of tremendous turmoil—alcohol or drug abuse, parental strife, divorce, or lack of communication. One after another, the children described feeling that nobody cared about them and that nobody had time to listen to their problems or to help when they were confused or frightened. They became convinced that they must be bad—"ugly," "garbage"— to deserve such neglect. A wall of surface toughness went up to hold in their anger and to protect themselves from being hurt any further. "Nobody was going to get close to me," one young man said. "I didn't trust a soul," said another.

The more angry the children became, the tougher they acted. Many beat up whoever got in their way: a friend, a parent, a teacher. Others attempted suicide. All agreed that getting into drugs was a form of suicide, too.

As the interviews went on, I saw the wall of

toughness fall away. At first, I heard vivid descriptions, filled with curse words and street language, of each addict's life on drugs. However, my question about their worst experience on drugs toned everyone down. After recalling that horrific event, each person opened up and shared the more sensitive part of themselves. Two young men cried, and young women who had just finished bragging about their sexual encounters admitted to feeling unloved and unwanted.

When their trust in me deepened, the eight addicts separately recounted wishing for rules and guidelines to follow as signs of parental love. Drugs, they said, became the only friend they could depend on, even though drugs contributed more to their loneliness.

For me, writing this book was an experience in making choices. I had to decide whether or not to include the graphic language of the interviewees and how vividly to describe the enormous troubles in these young addicts' lives. While I wanted my book to be true to its subjects and to the reality of drug abuse, I strongly felt, as an author and a parent, that I had to be selective in both language and details. Therefore, I intentionally excluded graphic language and scenes of a sexual nature. In some cases, I have also simplified the abuses in a child's life so that, for instance, effects of parental alcoholism did not become another theme in this book. This kind of selectivity was also necessary to make each person's life distinct and distinctive.

While I heard many shocking stories, what surprised me most was how long the parents and the schools denied that drugs were a problem. For whatever reason, they accepted the lies the children told them. Turning to individual counseling didn't appear to help much either, for the children lied to the therapists as well, tending to feel that they were being singled out as family troublemakers. Now, after treatment, the addicts say that drug addiction is a family problem that everyone has to work on together.

Unfortunately, most drug addicts of all ages don't go into treatment, and of those who do, many drop out after the first week. As the stories in this book make clear, it takes great determination to get off drugs and stay off. And staying off is not easy, particularly when peers or parents (or both) continue to abuse drugs.

Most young people in the presence of their peers just experiment with drugs. A smaller, but sizeable percentage, abuse drugs and become dependent on them. Too late, they realize they have an addictive personality. Clearly, everyone is a candidate to become a drug addict.

The young people who have been part of this book are proud of what they've accomplished. At the same time, they are careful not to be smug about their achievement. Looming in the background is always the fear they might one day be tempted to return to drugs. For them, the future will always be measured in small, but significant steps.

MAXINE B. ROSENBERG

FEBRUARY 1991

CHAPTER 1

GETTING STARTED

"NONE OF MY RELATIVES are alcoholics, drug addicts, foodaholics, overworkers, or gamblers," says twenty-one-year-old Rob. "In fact, most people looking at my home life from the outside would describe it as ideal.

"My parents have been married to each other for many years and always spent lots of time with their children. Even though my mother, a homemaker, was involved with all kinds of volunteer work, she was usually around when I came in from school. She's the kind of mother who kept the snack drawer filled with cookies and crackers for after-school treats.

"My father, a physician, always earned a good

salary, so money never was a problem in our family. We lived in a nice house in a wealthy suburb, and on holidays, we took vacations at beach resorts.

"I'm my parents' only son and the oldest of the three kids. As long as I can remember, I've known I was bright and that my intelligence made my parents and grandfather proud of me. Since most of my relatives are tremendously smart and high achievers, getting good grades was expected of me, too. The moment I started school, I felt under constant pressure to succeed. This set me apart from kids my age. At ten years old, I thought I'd have to be an astronaut, quarterback for the Dallas Cowboys, and the president of the United States to satisfy my parents. Of course, if asked, they would have said they just wanted me to be happy.

"Up until fifth grade, I was a model student whom teachers praised and classmates nicknamed The Brain. Not only was I smart, I was an excellent athlete, and good-looking, too. At that time, I thought I was perfect.

"Then one day while I was playing kickball, a kid called me fat. I wasn't fat at all, but the word threw me. Nobody had ever said anything bad about me before. A few days later, someone called me a nerd. Suddenly, I realized that maybe I wasn't so great. Maybe I had been wearing imaginary armor and now it was crushing me. Whatever, I got so scared. I couldn't believe that kids weren't accepting me.

"The worst part was not having anybody I could go to. Because we didn't talk about feelings in my family, I grew up keeping things to myself. So when all this started exploding, I stuffed my feelings inside.

"Meanwhile, I stopped studying and doing my homework, so kids would no longer label me a grind. When I had to read aloud in class, I purposely stumbled over words and called answers out of turn. But no matter how hard I tried to do badly, I still got As on my report card.

"Then in seventh grade I overheard a conversation between two girls. My name was mentioned about the school dance. The good-looking girl said, 'Go with him? Ah, man. He's horrible.'

"I couldn't believe what I'd heard. If she had taken a hammer and smashed me on the head, I don't think she could have hurt me more. At that moment, I felt as if I didn't fit in anywhere."

Soon after this conversation Rob got drunk for the first time. "My best friend and I raided his family's liquor cabinet and got so plastered. The next morning I had such a terrible hangover, but I didn't mind.

"The following weekend I got drunk again, and the weekend after that, too. In fact, whenever I slept at this friend's house, it became the pattern. We'd wait until his parents went to sleep, and then we'd drink as we watched TV. I never just had one glass. It always was to the extreme.

"Starting in ninth grade I went with another friend to a field where juniors and seniors held after-school keg parties. At first when I saw all the older classmen, I was nervous. But once I'd had a few drinks with them, I felt real cool. These guys accepted me.

"From then on I went to these keg parties a couple of times a week, always leaving drunk, yet craving more. So every morning, before my parents awoke, I made myself a screwdriver and would go to my first period class buzzed. For the rest of the day I'd think about getting drunk again. School was the last thing on my mind.

"At the keg parties, people also smoked pot. In the spring of ninth grade I decided to try some when the pipe was passed around. In the beginning I didn't like the way pot made me feel, but I kept trying it whenever it was offered, and soon I got into it. It wasn't long before I was smoking pot every day. I always smoked it when I was drunk and with another person.

"That summer I changed my friends from the guys who were academic achievers to those who got high and liked drinking. Anytime someone from the old crowd would meet me, he'd say, 'I can't believe what you're doing.'

"Compared to most addicts I've met, I started late. But in the end, I became just as addicted as anyone else."

Eighteen-year-old Pat's life couldn't seem more different on the surface from Rob's. "I grew up surrounded by people who were addicts," Pat re-

Pat, today: *"I spent so much energy worrying about my sisters that I didn't take care of myself."*

calls. "Both of my parents are addicted to drugs. My father, who was in and out of jail before he even married my mother, was on heroin. And my mother would take whatever drugs she could get her hands on.

"When we'd celebrate Christmas and Easter at my grandparents' on my father's side, everyone would get drunk, including my grandfather, who didn't drink the rest of the year. On these holidays it was amazing if my father showed up at all.

"The year I was four, my parents separated. And when I was eight, they divorced. On the day their marriage ended, my father said to me, 'Now you're the man of the house,' and I took his words literally.

"From that moment on I felt I was responsible for my twin sisters, who were four years younger than me. I thought it was my duty to keep them safe from my mother's boyfriends, who sexually abused them and me, too. Added to this, I tried to protect them from our own father's beatings. I spent so much energy worrying about my sisters that I didn't take care of myself.

"In my house drugs were used so much that no one noticed when I started taking them, the same year my parents divorced. When I saw that everybody in my house smoked joints, I was curious to try them, too. One day my mother's boyfriend took me with him to the school yard to buy drugs. As he was making a deal, some teenagers offered me a joint. The first hit didn't do anything to me, but that didn't stop me from smoking pot again and again over the next two years. By age ten I was getting high from pot all the time.

"Meanwhile, when I was nine, my mother moved all of us to an upstate commune where we lived with thirty other people—bikers, left-over hippies, and Hell's Angels. From then on I was bounced from one house to another. If I wasn't living with my mother, I was with my father, or my grandmother, or my great-grandmother. Each time I'd be told to leave because I caused too much trouble, or when I thought things got rough, I'd take off on my own. Except for one year when we three kids were with our father, and six months when we lived with our grandmother, my sisters stayed with our mother. But because our mother was emotionally unstable, they too moved around a lot. Every move meant changing schools. Probably that's why teachers never knew us well or noticed the bruises we had from all the beatings.

"In school I'd sit quietly, not knowing what was going on. Part of this was because I was high, but I also felt stupid, since I couldn't read or write. (Finally, in seventh grade, I was found to have serious learning problems.)

"Through the school years I mostly stayed by myself. If someone got in my way, though, I'd go into a rage, where I'd throw a chair or hit the person. It didn't even matter if it was the teacher.

"My grandmother, who for a long time knew about her daughter's drug problem, wanted to protect my sisters and me. One day after Mom moved us to the commune, she brought the three of us to her house to live with her. I cried because I couldn't understand why we couldn't be with our mother. I never saw anything wrong with our life. Although my eyes were black and blue from being hit, I thought that was what was supposed to happen to women and children.

"For the next six months we stayed with our grandmother as she tried to get custody of us through the courts. But she couldn't gather enough evidence to show the police how abused and neglected we were. Finally she lost the case, and we went home to our mother again.

"On my tenth birthday I was back in the commune. Naturally, there was no party, since everybody there was high. To celebrate, though, my mother offered me a joint. She said she knew I was smoking pot with kids on the street and would rather I did it with her. I thought, this is cool!

"A few days later I had some friends over. While we were smoking pot, we heard my mother come in. Quickly, my friends tried to hide their joints, but I told them not to bother. I said knowing my mother, she wouldn't mind. And I was right. As soon as she saw I had a joint, she took a hit. The guys were amazed. I said to them, 'Doesn't your mother get high with you?', thinking this kind of stuff went on in all families.

"The odd thing is that I never realized my family

was different from others. I grew up believing that every family was surrounded by total craziness. Not until I was into treatment did I learn different."

Kerry, who's fifteen, comes from a wealthy family of professionals that is respected in the community. Alcoholism is common on both sides of her family. "Many of my relatives have problems with drinking—and drugs—and no one thinks anything's wrong with offering alcohol to the kids. When my younger sister was four, my father gave her a beer. Two years later, at our family's annual Christmas party, she got plastered. None of the adults seemed to notice because they were too busy getting drunk themselves.

"The minute I tasted alcohol, I loved it. At every opportunity I would finish off any liquor my parents left in their glasses. By age nine I had already gotten drunk a number of times, always at family gatherings.

"When I was eleven, I was starting my school day with a drink. Either my friend or I would carry a bottle in a purse, or we hid one in a paper towel roll in the school bathroom. Two years before this started, my parents had separated, and now they had just divorced. I was feeling real bad then, blaming myself for their marriage ending. At least drinking gave me a boost. And liquor also freed my writing and artwork.

"Around this time I also started inhaling when I smoked cigarettes. In the past I'd swipe them from my father, but never that many. Now I was up to a pack or more a day."

On the weekends Kerry went to parties where she and her friends would help themselves to the liquor from the parents' bar, or they'd ask older brothers and sisters to buy them some. "At one of these parties, a kid brought pot, and someone else had a rolling paper. Within seconds all of us ran onto the driveway to roll the joint. As we carefully passed it around, I took a hit. Nothing happened.

" 'This is no fun,' I told everyone. Then suddenly I screamed, 'Oh my God! I feel it!' I couldn't stop laughing. And I felt dizzy. I must have looked so stupid.

"A month later I was offered pot again, this time

by my friend's sister's boyfriend. The four of us were sitting on the couch when the boyfriend asked if I smoked pot. 'Sure,' I said. 'I've done enough to know how to handle everything.' He then passed the bowl to me, and I, being so innocent, didn't know where to put my finger. Finally he showed me. The stuff he'd brought was potent. After four or five hits, I floated. From then on, I really started rolling."

Like Kerry, John also comes from a family that has money, a nice house, and addiction problems. His father, an alcoholic, died when John was a baby. And when his mother remarried, her second husband was addicted, too. And abusive.

"As far back as I can remember, my stepfather, whom I called Dad, beat me, but he never touched his three kids, who lived with us. Sometimes I'd call the police if he hit me real hard. But because I had no bruises to show, the police didn't do a thing. Once they'd leave, my father and I would avoid each other for a week. During that time, nobody in the family discussed the abuse incident. It was ignored, just like Dad's drinking.

"Even though my stepfather drank a lot, he warned me not to touch alcohol. Of course, this made me more curious about it, since my older brother was drinking, too. I kept wondering, what is this taboo liquor all men take religiously? Starting at age seven I'd sip whatever the adults left in their glasses after a party. The stuff tasted disgusting, and I'd spit it out. But a few weeks later I'd try some again, thinking that's what it takes to be a man. I want to be macho like my father, convinced that then he would accept me.

"As it turned out, I never liked alcohol that much, although in junior high, I once got very drunk and went out of control at my friend's house. What bothered me about drinking were the advertisements I would see on TV. They linked alcohol with fatal car accidents, and this scared me. As for taking drugs, I don't ever remember any ads then that said 'Pot kills!' or 'Cocaine kills!' So I thought they were fine."

The first time John tried pot, he was eight. "I had noticed that every afternoon my thirteen-year-old brother and his friends climbed up a tree and would sit there for hours. One day I decided to see what they were doing. To reward myself for getting to the top, I asked my brother if I could smoke whatever he was passing around. He handed me the joint, and for the next forty-five minutes, I laughed so hard. To this day I don't know how I got back down to the ground.

"Afterward, when the pot started wearing off, I felt so tired. But I didn't care. It was worth it to have been with the older guys. More than that, pot made me forget my anger toward my father.

"From that first joint through junior high school, I smoked pot about thirty or forty more times— always with friends, never again with my brother, who had stopped using drugs early on and was more into drinking. During the school day, I would do my work, then later reward myself by getting high. Just a few hits was enough to get my mind off my home life."

Chapter 2

THE "GOOD TIMES"

MEANWHILE, John's anger about his home life kept mounting. In school his grades got worse, and he constantly argued with classmates. "Finally, when I was ten, my parents took me to a therapist to find out why I was acting so crazy. The therapist put me on medication to calm me down and had me come to see him once a week. I thought, at least now I have someone I can talk to and tell what it's like having an alcoholic parent. But every time I'd come home from the therapist's office, my father would question me about what I had said there. This made me tense and feel like I was being watched. After a few months the therapy stopped. I never understood why.

"By the time I was twelve, I was boiling over with rage. Although marijuana made me forget my problems for the moment, they were always there with me. Not only was I angry with my father, I was infuriated because I had to repeat seventh grade. I fought back by wearing black clothes and letting my hair grow long. In school I became the bad guy, carving satanic graffiti on desks and writing on bathroom walls, while around the neighborhood, my friends and I threw smoke bombs and rocks into people's windows. To outsiders though, my family looked fine—except for me.

"Now my parents brought me to another therapist, whom I stayed with for about four years. I told this therapist, too, about my father's drinking and the beatings, and he called in my parents. No sooner did I give my side of the story than my father would disagree with what I had said. Calmly, my father would deny his drinking problem, while I'd be screaming that it wasn't so. Out of frustration, I finally said, 'Forget it' and dropped the whole thing. Naturally, I never told the therapist about *my* drug problem."

As soon as John entered high school, he smoked marijuana more frequently. And he found a new group of friends. "I'd go into the woods and meet high school seniors there who had pot. They'd pass the pipe to me, and I'd take a hit. Getting along with these big guys made me feel real cool—more like a man.

"The minute I'd get out of school, I'd get stoned. Later, at home, when I tried to do my homework, my eyes would close. But I didn't care. At least when I was high, I could put my father out of my mind.

"Soon I began taking drugs during the school day. And on weekends my friends and I would pool our money and have pot parties. Each time I'd get high, I'd tell everyone how awesome I felt. But I could also see myself and the guys getting hooked on the stuff. So I told my friends, 'We've got to be careful, or we'll get too into this and end up like the burned-out seniors who are dealing.' My friends and I made a vow to keep an eye on one another, and we shook on it. The vow went out the window."

When John was on marijuana, his interests came

second to everyone else's. Pot made him totally lose sight of who he was and what he enjoyed. "Instead of drawing and writing poetry, which I loved, I spent my time trying to please others. I thought that if I made people happy, they would like me. If someone laughed at my jokes, I'd tell more. If a kid asked me to get high with him, I'd do that, too.

"What concerned me most was being a man. While I hated fighting, I knew I'd have to do that to impress the guys I hung out with. One time at the mall some huge guy started up with me. I was so scared that I thought I would vomit. With all my friends there, watching, I felt I couldn't back out. In the end, the guy flattened me."

At John's suburban school there was no problem getting drugs. The dealers were always around selling the stuff. "Every week I took my allowance and used it up at one shot to buy a twenty-five-dollar bag of pot, which a group of us would smoke in a car on the school parking lot.

"When teachers would come by, we'd roll down the windows and talk to them. They knew what was going on from the smell of the pot, yet all they said to us was 'Get to class.' We thought they were so cool for not reporting us. Now when I think about it, I get so angry. Those teachers didn't even care that we were stoned.

"Around this time my father became suspicious of what I was up to. More than once he told me that my eyes were red from pot and that I stunk from it. Right away my mother would come to my defense and say to Dad, 'John's only experimenting. It's just a phase.' My acting like a good little boy in front of her had her convinced that I was clean."

Danielle was twelve the first time she tried drugs. She was with her sister, Jennifer, at a party, celebrating the marriage of a family friend's daughter, Susan. "Since I was young, Jennifer and I have been very close. Although she's two years older than me, I hung out with her a lot and thought that she and her friends were big shots. Jennifer had already smoked pot with her friends, but she had never offered me any. So when this guy Tony at the party said he had some, I said, 'Ooo, I've always wanted to try that.' Jennifer, Tony, and I then went outside and smoked a big joint. I took one hit and said, "Whoa, this is heavy!' A few more hits got me major-league stoned.

"That night I smoked some more joints and drank a whole lot, too. I couldn't stand up and had a terrible headache, but I refused to go to sleep. There was no way I was going to miss out on the fun.

"In the beginning I loved the sensation pot gave me. Although I'd feel awful the next day, I wanted to do it again and again. Drugs made me feel carefree, as if I had nothing to worry about. And in my family, there was plenty that made me furious. For one, Susan, who lived on and off with us, used to disrupt our house whenever she was around. When Susan wasn't there, my sister and I argued with our mother. While Jennifer would quickly apologize and get quiet after each scene, I'd go out of control. To keep out of things, my father watched TV."

Even before drugs, Danielle followed whatever other kids did. "If my friends became rock 'n roll heads, so did I. If they wore motorcycle boots and black leather jackets, I copied. I'd do anything so

Danielle, today: *"I'd do anything so I wouldn't have to be alone."*

I wouldn't have to be alone. For a long time I loved to ice skate and draw, but once I got in with the drug crowd, I gave them both up, just to hang out with the guys.

"Right before my freshman year my family bought a house in a wealthy suburb, whose school system is supposed to be one of the best in the country. In a matter of a few days, I met some cool metal heads and burn-outs, and immediately I became one of them. Up till this point, I had been getting B pluses and Cs in school. But once I started hanging out with this crowd, school no longer mattered. I'd cut classes and go to the park to get high with them.

"When I did come to class, I'd be stoned and sit in the back of the room, where teachers couldn't see me. The next day I'd bring in a forged note with my parent's signature, excusing my lateness or absence. No one, not my teachers or parents, suspected what I was up to. It was amazing how easy it was for me to get away with things."

By the time Kerry was twelve, she started losing her neighborhood friends. "They kept away from me when they found out about the alcohol and drugs. At least when I visited Dad, I had fast kids to hang around with. It wasn't long before I started dressing like them. Until then, people had called me Miss Sunshine because of the way I looked and acted—like an innocent little girl. Then I totally changed. I started wearing tight jeans, concert T-shirts, and loads of makeup.

"Meanwhile, I was drinking and smoking pot more than ever. Pretty soon I got involved with a new crowd at home, too. Like my friends at Dad's, these kids accepted me and made me feel I was being protected. Although I was the youngest among them, they told me that I was beautiful and a great kid. I loved hearing that, but I also worried that maybe they let me hang around them because I always carried five or ten dollars in my purse and would give it to them to buy pot.

"Soon my mother noticed my new friends and got very worried. So she brought me to a therapist. Mom didn't think I was involved with drugs, but she suspected that Daryl, the boy I liked, was on them.

Kerry, today: *"When I visited Dad, I had fast kids to hang around with. It wasn't long before I started dressing like them. Up till then, people had called me Miss Sunshine because of the way I looked and acted—like an innocent little girl."*

"I never told the therapist about my drinking and drugs. If I talked at all it was about my parents' divorce and how it bothered me.

"At that time it would have been hard for my mother to know exactly what was going on. She couldn't get any idea from a change in my school grades, since I had never done well. And while I was always exhausted from pot, she didn't see me that way, because she came home late from her job as a dental hygienist.

"I was glad my mother didn't know about the drugs and that she didn't bring up the drinking. If I had gotten caught, it all would have been over."

At nine years old, Donna smoked cigarettes and drank beer and liquor. Two years later she was using marijuana. "My friend Karen and I were given some joints by a guy we knew. Neither of us was sure how to use them, so the first time, we smoked them away from everyone else, not wanting to look stupid. We got really stoned, and our cheeks hurt from laughing. Then we went to Pancake House and pigged out.

"I grew up in a family where there was constant arguing. When I was six months old, my parents separated, although they didn't divorce until I was sixteen. Through the years my father lived on and off with us, or we all moved in with him. It was really hard for my sister, Laura, and me. My parents kept trying to make their marriage work, but there was too much bitterness between them. We grew up hearing them fight all the time.

"The year I was ten my mother's boyfriend, an alcoholic, moved in with the family. As soon as my mother came home from work, she'd ask me to make her a Southern Comfort on the rocks to help her unwind. Later in the evening the two of them would drink some more.

"After a while I wanted to drink with them, too. So I also started sitting with Mom's boyfriend and having a beer, and Mom thought this was cute.

"By sixth grade, I was drinking with friends. And I smoked pot with them, too. Before that time, I had been doing extremely well in school, but in sixth grade, forget it!

"At first I'd only smoke pot with my friend Karen.

Then different friends in the park would offer me joints, and I'd say, 'What the heck!' I didn't go around looking for joints. They were always there. If I wanted marijuana and, later, cocaine, I could have them in a snap. When you're doing drugs, you find out who all the dealers are, and usually there are a lot in every town.

"Soon I was smoking pot at home. To make sure my mother wouldn't find out, I offered some to my sister, knowing if she got involved, she wouldn't tell on me. I'd say to Laura, who was then nine, 'Try some. It's good.' And she'd take a hit."

"By now I had changed my friends, no longer hanging out with the smart, popular girls I used to like. Instead I looked for guys on drugs, who had big family problems. With them, I felt less different."

When Cindy was ten, she saw her father smoke marijuana with his friends. "I thought, if my father smoked pot in front of me, it must be okay. So when my girlfriend sneaked some roaches from her brother and handed me a couple, I smoked them, even though I had promised myself never to do anything more than drink beer. Almost immediately I became addicted to pot, the way I had become addicted to cigarettes and alcohol a few years earlier.

"From the beginning, pot made me think I was in fantasy land. When I smoked it, I couldn't stop laughing, and all I wanted to do was eat. Pot also numbed my angry feelings about my family life.

"Neither my mother nor father was ever around much to take care of my sister, Liz, and me. Although my father lived nearby after my parents divorced, he was very unpredictable because, like so many of our relatives, he drank and took drugs. My mother also drank a lot, but she managed to hold two and three jobs at a time to earn enough money to buy a car and put food on the table. Yet she couldn't find a moment to listen to her kids' problems.

"Going way back, I grew up feeling different from kids my age. I went to a Catholic school, where divorce was frowned upon, and that made things even harder. To make matters worse, I was left back in first grade. For years I was taller than everyone else in class. All this made me so angry that I started beating kids up, especially girls who didn't want me for a friend."

As soon as Cindy got into marijuana, she challenged whomever she was with to smoke more joints than she. "I always liked to compete. At first it was in sports. Then it started with drinking and drugs. Even though I'd get stomach pains and headaches from overdoing it, I had to prove that I was better than everyone else.

"By the time I was eleven, I smoked pot every day. On weekends I'd go roller-skating with friends and take a hit at the rink. Drugs were always on my mind.

"A year later my mother found some pot in the house and asked me whose it was. I said I was holding it for my friend, and she bought the story. I couldn't believe that my mother would let me get away with it. Yet I should have known better. For so long, my mother closed her eyes to whatever I was into. And my father wasn't any different.

"Meanwhile, my sister, Liz, who never touched

drugs, knew I was getting more and more into trouble. She kept telling me that if I didn't change, I'd end up a total mess like some of the friends I hung out with. Whenever she'd say that, I'd go into a fury, because she had insulted kids I liked. Nobody was going to tell me what to do, not at home, or in school.

"If teachers tried to discipline me, I'd have temper tantrums, and then they'd call my mother about my behavior problem. Even when my mother brought me to a therapist, I refused to say one word about the drinking and drug use that went on in our family. It was our secret. Not even my grandma knew about her daughter's drinking and all the chaos we lived with."

Four years before Jeff started drinking and taking drugs, his parents separated. Following the separation, Jeff lived with his mother for several years while his older brother, Ismael, stayed with their father.

"When I was twelve my mother moved in with a friend, and I went back to live with my dad. He made me sweep and mop the floors, do the laundry, and help prepare dinner, while my brother only had to wash the dishes. Ismael was considered the intelligent one, and I was the black sheep who was always in trouble. Only my grandmother, who visited us from Puerto Rico a few times a year, made me feel good. At my dad's it was no fun with all the chores I had, and my brother acting like he was so smart. Whenever I could, I'd get out of the house and get drunk with my friend Junior.

"About then I also got into drugs, first given to me by my older cousin, who came by a lot. She was real cool and danced well, and I wanted to be part of her world. Like so many other people in my family who got hooked onto things, I didn't realize addiction could happen to me.

"Meanwhile, I was still passing all my subjects and behaving pretty well. I didn't smoke cigarettes around the school building, let alone come to class drunk or high. The friends I had were the kind who did homework during free periods and helped me when I had problems with a subject.

"So nobody could tell what I was up to. Since my

brother and I barely spoke, he didn't seem to notice anything. Nor did my parents. Although I worked afternoons in my father's automobile repair shop, he suspected nothing. From the way I dressed—in a shirt, tie, and slacks—I looked like an innocent kid."

In the beginning, Jeff's cousin only brought marijuana to the house. But then she started bringing cocaine. "Crack hadn't come out yet, so we freebased cocaine in the basement. At first it didn't give me much of a high, but after I did it a number of times, I felt the rush to my head, and I loved that feeling. Still, when my cousin didn't bring drugs, I wasn't about to run out and buy them. And I continued to do fine in school. I didn't fail, I didn't fight, and I didn't steal. I thought I was in control.

"But by the fall of sophomore year I was a different person, who dressed in black leather and wore gold chains and a gold pinky ring. The friends I hung around with now smoked pot during lunch and listened to rap music.

"I became so defiant that in class I talked back to teachers, then refused to take detention. One day I burned my test paper when I found out I had failed an exam. Soon after, the school expelled me. They said I was dealing drugs, but I wasn't. When my father heard the news, he really got on my case."

CHAPTER 3

WHO CARES?

THAT AUTUMN Jeff enrolled in another private school. From the start he cut classes to meet a friend and get drunk. "I was furious at everything, even my old school, for making me leave. One afternoon I went back there and walked right into the Spanish class led by the teacher who had given me all the detentions. I went up and down the aisles, shaking hands with the kids and saying, 'Yo, what's up, man?' Everybody thought I was crazy. The dean called the police and also notified the school I was enrolled in. Soon after I was expelled from that school, too.

"Now my head was really confused. I was back living with my mother again. And I thought that no one cared about me. Only my cousin who gave me the drugs knew how I felt. She would tell my father, who would say to her that he loved me. But I never heard those words from him.

"At that point I began to buy bags of marijuana, and I sniffed cocaine with friends. Nothing mattered anymore. My attitude was, who cares!

"Thinking I'd do better in a new environment, my mother decided we should move out of state. But there I found kids who were worse than any I'd ever been with before. Not only did they do drugs, they stole and dismantled cars just for fun, which I went along with.

"I began drinking and smoking marijuana every day, besides using cocaine. In the morning I'd come into school stoned. Without knowing it, I was addicted. I'd give my mother some of the money I got from my after-school job, and the rest I'd use to buy drugs. I knew my life was getting worse, but I didn't care.

"After living out of state for a year, my mother and I moved back to our old neighborhood. By then I was sixteen and heavily hooked on drugs. My friend Raoul and I competed to see who could get the most. Since crack had just come out, we'd buy that with money we got from our jobs. Or I'd steal.

"Once I got arrested for taking a car and had to spend two nights in jail. When my mother took me out on bail, she said, 'Wait until your father hears.' He took one look at me and cried, 'My son, my son, my beautiful son.' I thought he was putting on an act because I was so used to him being tough with me. Still, I promised him I wouldn't do anything wrong again. The next day I was out puffing a joint."

When Donna was in seventh grade, a girl she knew from town offered her a joint. "Since I had been smoking marijuana for a year, I said okay without thinking about it. After one hit, my whole body went numb. 'What's in this?' I asked, and the girl said, 'Angel dust.' I should have known it wasn't marijuana from the smell, but I was already too drunk from beer to think straight. That night I came home so wasted.

"With another girlfriend, who had tried it before,

I also used mescaline. She had asked me if I wanted to trip out with her, and although I was scared by the bad stories I had heard about the drug, I said yes.

"That year I took LSD, too. Had I known beforehand what I was taking, I wouldn't have tried it. When I came home that night, I was so out of it that I fell down a flight of stairs. My sister, Laura, looked at me and said, 'What's wrong with you?' I just smiled, not aware of anything.

"I'm sure by then my mother knew I was into drugs, but she did nothing to change things. If she asked me about the joints she found in my room, I would tell her they were my boyfriend's, and she'd let it go. My mother's the type of person who can't believe someone in her family would do anything wrong.

"Since my father was hardly around, he wasn't very effective, either. The times he didn't like what I was into, he'd say to my mother, 'Your daughter needs help.' Then the two of them would have a big fight.

"So I basically grew up knowing I could do what-

Donna, today: *"I basically grew up knowing I could do whatever I wanted."*

ever I wanted. At thirteen I'd smoke joints at home, not even caring if I was caught. Once my mother smelled the pot and called from her room, 'Put out that cigarette!' I shouted back, 'Don't tell me what to do!' Nobody was going to stop *me* from using marijuana. When I smoked it, I felt happier than I had ever been.

"At seven o'clock every night I'd leave the house to go to the park, where I'd meet the guys to drink and smoke pot. With the drug crowd I felt I belonged. We made up our own family of people who cared about and understood one another. Through the years we pretty much stayed together."

Day after day the abuse in Pat's house continued. As he tried to protect his sisters, he'd get hurt. "I became so full of hate that I didn't want to live. Once, while high on marijuana, I stepped in front of a car.

"By the time I was ten, I was getting stoned every day. Either my mother would give me pot, or I'd just take it from her.

"Meanwhile, I stayed away from the commune

as much as I could. A friend I hung out with knew I loved sports, so together we joined the county wrestling team. To me it was just another way to get out my anger.

"About then my mother started to fall apart emotionally and couldn't take care of the three of us together. So she'd send me to my grandmother's for a few days, while my sisters stayed at home. It upset me to leave my sisters, knowing what could happen to them.

"More than once, the police had come to the commune and arrested people, including my mother. Sometimes I wouldn't see her for days. I'd walk around in a numb state, asking everybody, 'Where is she?' I felt so lost without her there and was convinced that these awful things were happening because I was bad. At twelve, I tried to hang myself, but it didn't work.

Soon after Pat started taking Valium and speed to block out his feelings. He also took cocaine, thinking he deserved the depressed mood the drug left him with when the rush wore off. Then he moved on to crack, mescaline, and angel dust.

"When I was almost thirteen, my mother was hospitalized for emotional problems, so my sisters and I went to live with our father. He was in a methadone program trying to stop his heroin habit, while I was getting high all the time. It made him furious to see that I wasn't about to get off drugs. One day at three A.M. he threw me out of the house. Immediately I called my grandmother—my mother's mother—who came to get me. The next day, she put me on a plane for Florida to stay with her mother. She thought I'd be better off away from my parents.

"Today I understand that she was trying to help me, but back then I thought she was just another person wanting me out of her life. It seemed that everyone I knew tried to get rid of me. There was no one I could trust or get close to."

At age thirteen, Cindy took handfuls of caffeine pills, hoping they'd make her get thinner and be a better athlete. "Sports was the only thing that got me a lot of attention. I was especially good in basketball and softball, and cheerleading, too, which

I did on weekends. But all the drugs I was taking messed me up. If it wasn't pot, then it was alcohol, or speed, or mescaline, or hash, or cocaine, or angel dust. I even smoked crack. In fact I did everything except heroin. My stomach was such a wreck that I couldn't eat. In freshman year, instead of going to parochial school, I went to a public high school, where I thought I'd be much happier. If ever I could change, I was sure it would be now. But as soon as the kids saw my stoned-out, hippy look, they asked if I wanted to smoke a joint with them. It took me a minute to decide. Yes!

"On the other hand, my sister, Liz, acted the exact opposite from me. She preferred to isolate herself in her room with books while I ran out to find friends to get high with.

"From the beginning my father gave me a lot of drugs. As time passed we started doing them together. I felt that he and I were into the same thing, with Liz on the outside. But I used my father, just like I used everybody else. All I cared about was what I could get from people. If one friend had more money than the next, I'd drop the first, thinking I could get more drugs with the other. What mattered most was when and how I'd get my next high."

As soon as Rob started drinking and smoking marijuana regularly, his school grades dropped to Bs and Cs. "My parents suspected something was wrong and asked how they could help. I promised them, and myself, too, that I would do better. But like a guy who has a bad hangover and says, 'I'll never take another drink,' I was back on drugs and alcohol soon after.

"Now my parents tell me they had some idea that I was drinking, but they believed all teenagers experimented, so they didn't make a fuss about it. As for the drugs, that never entered their minds. If I came home as a Martian, they would have found that more believable.

"By tenth grade I was taking acid, a very powerful drug which caused me to hallucinate and think in weird ways. It made me feel that I was bad and going in the opposite direction from studying, which is exactly what I wanted. That same year I used coke, too, and I also started selling drugs.

"The guidance counselor at school wondered why my grades were slipping and called me down to his office. I told him I hated being at school, and he reported that to my parents. That's when they decided to send me to a therapist. Every week I'd go to counseling and find something to talk about. I told the therapist I sometimes drank, but I never mentioned my drug problem. After a while I felt the therapy was getting me nowhere, so I quit.

"By the end of sophomore year I had failed every subject. On my report card, teachers wrote, 'I don't know what to do to help him.'

"Now when I came home drunk every night, my parents lectured to me on the spot. They told me I was doing something very serious to myself. But still drugs weren't on their mind. By being sneaky, I was able to get over on them.

"The summer before eleventh grade my parents told me that I had to go to boarding school when the new school year started. They said that not only had I failed every course in the public high school, I also was a bad influence on my sisters. (A couple of times I had given Randy, who was eight, sips of tequila, which I thought was funny, but she and Dorothy, who was eleven, were mad. They didn't know what to make of me.)

"Still, I was furious that I was being sent away. I felt my parents were shipping me out so they could have it easier. It was as if they had read a manual that said, 'Get rid of your kid if he's having trouble in school.'

"At the same time I wouldn't have accepted anything they would have suggested. All I wanted was to drink and do drugs. I pushed away their love and kept a distance from them and my sisters, too.

"During the first trimester at boarding school, I managed to stay sober. I was afraid that if I got caught, my parents would find out about my drug problem. But when I was home on weekends, I'd party with friends, drinking, taking acid, or smoking opium and pot. I also tried mescaline and LSD, without realizing exactly what they were. The guy in the city who sold me drugs gave them to me.

"Meanwhile, on school days, I became so desperate to get high that I'd drink two six-ounce bottles of mouthwash for its alcohol content. It tasted pretty terrible, but it had the effect of strong liquor."

A month or so after Danielle got involved with marijuana, she and her sister, Jennifer, along with their friend Judy, bought mescaline, a psychedelic drug that causes hallucination. "Judy had a dealer friend at school who got us the stuff. With my twenty-dollars-a-week allowance, I had just enough to pay for it.

"The first time we tried it, Jennifer really tripped out, but I felt nothing. Within a couple of weeks, though, I was heavy into the drug. Whenever I took mescaline it made me laugh like crazy and see weird swirls and bright colors. I thought this was so neat, but I hated the bugs I imagined crawling all over the place. Still, I kept buying the stuff. When I couldn't get it at school, Jennifer and I would go into the city.

"By now, twenty dollars couldn't buy me what I wanted. So I'd steal money from my mother's wallet. Since she never was quite sure how much she had at one time, she didn't realize anything was

missing. In school I stole, too—portable tape play-
ers, watches, and radios that kids left outside their
lockers. I'd sell these things to other people so I'd
have more money.

"One day when the mail came, my sister and I
each got two thousand dollars from our grandfather, who's very wealthy. He wrote a card that
said he couldn't remember when our birthdays
were, so here was a gift in case they had passed.
Jennifer and I thought a miracle had happened.
With the money we were able to buy a lot of drugs.
But in less than a month and a half, nothing was
left."

As Danielle got deeper and deeper into drugs,
she never took the time to think about why she
might be doing this to herself. "If I got into a slump,
I would go out and do drugs. It didn't even matter
what kinds they were. I was such a garbage head
that I'd use anything that was around.

"One day when I was in a store with my mother,
I got caught for shoplifting. My mother got me off
the hook, but even then, she and my father didn't
figure out the real problem. They thought I was
just a wild kid who had trouble fitting in."

A GALLERY OF ABUSE

Laying a line of cocaine on a mirror.

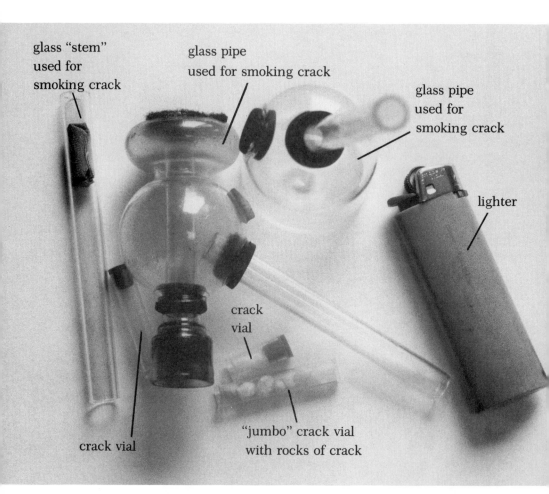

glass "stem"
used for
smoking crack

glass pipe
used for smoking crack

glass pipe
used for
smoking crack

lighter

crack
vial

crack vial

"jumbo" crack vial
with rocks of crack

Crack paraphernalia

Smoking crack

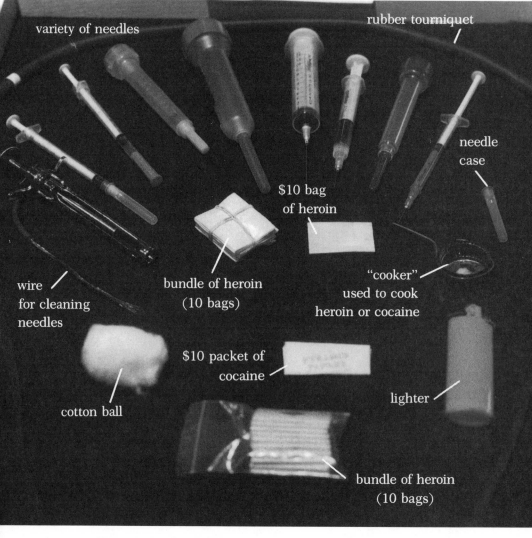

variety of needles

rubber tourniquet

needle
case

$10 bag
of heroin

wire
for cleaning
needles

bundle of heroin
(10 bags)

"cooker"
used to cook
heroin or cocaine

$10 packet of
cocaine

lighter

cotton ball

bundle of heroin
(10 bags)

Heroin paraphernalia

CHAPTER 4

BOTTOMING OUT

WHENEVER DANIELLE TOOK DRUGS, she felt good—until the drugs wore off. "I hated the low, depressed feelings drugs left me with. The longer I was on drugs, the worse it was coming down from them. The only way I could get rid of those awful feelings was to get high again.

"One night at a party when I was dusted, my sister took a hit off a joint. Suddenly Jennifer's body went numb. She looked like she was in a hypnotic state, sitting there, drooling. I screamed, 'Jennifer, wake up!' But she didn't respond. Thinking she had overdosed, I yelled, 'Somebody, do something quick!' No one moved because everybody was out of it. All alone, I carried my sister into the bedroom

59

and laid her down. Meanwhile, I hadn't even come to it myself, and here I was supposed to be helping her. I was so scared. To add to this, my friend Judy kept walking into the room, saying, 'What are we going to do with the body?'

"Jennifer awoke in an hour which to me had seemed like forever. She didn't remember anything that had gone on, but I'll never forget that experience. It was the worst I had on drugs. Jennifer was sixteen when it happened, and I was fourteen. The following week we both went out and got dusted again."

Still, every time Danielle thought about that evening, she felt frightened. "What stayed in my mind was how no one had come to help me. What if Jennifer had died? All the while I had thought I was cool knowing so many kids, but now I realized that these people were just hang-out dudes—not good friends I could count on.

"About then my mother insisted that the four of us go into family counseling, and my father agreed. They were concerned about my temper outbursts and how out of hand I would get when I was mad.

Also my mother now suspected that either my sister or I was taking money from her purse, and that worried her, too.

"We went to the therapist regularly, and for the first time, my mother set limits. I had to straighten my room once a week and be home at a certain time each night. But these rules didn't apply to Jennifer. Maybe she got off easier because she was older than me and because she kept her angry feelings to herself, while I exploded or ran away from home. Whatever, I felt like I was being singled out again and refused to do what my mother said. This led to bigger fights between the two of us.

"Finally, one evening, the therapist said I needed to be seen alone. I thought, now everybody thinks I'm crazy. During those private sessions, I wouldn't tell a thing."

At the same time that Kerry was changing friends, her use of marijuana was getting her into trouble. Often she'd fight with people while she was high but later have no memory of what had happened. "Once, a girl pulled a clump of hair from my head, and I didn't even feel it. During other blackouts I'd have sex with guys, and the next morning I wouldn't remember a thing.

"Still, I thought I was better off than many in my crowd. All the kids I hung out with were into higher drugs and were constantly running into the city to get them. I was only using alcohol and pot then, and I thought I was in complete control.

"But when I was fourteen, I tried to overdose on aspirin and Tylenol. Especially then, I was so down because many of the guys I liked were no longer around. Some were in jail, while others wanted nothing to do with me. At the same time my mother had found out I was stealing, so we weren't getting along. Nor was I on good terms with my father, who hit me a lot.

"One day in school I took some pills, but as soon as I realized I might die from an overdose, I told my friend Laurie. She ran to the nurse, who called an ambulance. When I was carried out, all my friends were lined up in the hallway to see how I was. That made me feel I was loved and cared about.

"After spending four days in a general hospital, I went to a psychiatric hospital for the next three months. Everyone—including my younger brother and sister—knew I had attempted suicide, but nobody could figure out *why* I had wanted to end my life. Even I wasn't sure what the *real* reason was. Maybe I was crying for attention.

"Anyhow, when my mother brought me to the hospital, she didn't know about the drugs. And neither did the hospital staff. They asked me if I took drugs, and I said never. They believed my story.

"During the three months in the hospital I had no alcohol, drugs, or cigarettes. At the school there my grades got better. But that New Years, when I went home on a weekend pass, I got stoned. A few weeks later I was discharged.

"Immediately I started using drugs again, getting high in my backyard while my mother was at work. For variety, I combined pot with cocaine. The pot would make me drowsy, and then the cocaine would take effect and give me a high. This going up and down at least was different, but it wasn't a lot of fun. I'd get terrible mood swings where one minute I'd be laughing and very lovey-dovey, and the next, I'd be bawling.

"Soon I started using powerful drugs all the time. With my boyfriend and one of my girlfriends, I'd mix angel dust with acid, then have chases of coke. This combination of drugs made me freak out. If I was in a parked car, I'd scream because I thought it was moving. Or I'd imagine that people were coming out of my cigarette smoke.

"By now I was stoned most of the day. My stomach was such a mess that even little bits of food made me throw up. I hardly went to school anymore.

"With all this going on, my mother still didn't confront me about drugs, although today she says she suspected them. Instead, my mother and I would get into terrible fights about everything else. When I felt I couldn't take it any more, I'd move in with a friend for a few weeks. At night my brother and sister would call to talk to me, but I'd be out until three in the morning. Anyhow, I didn't want to speak to them. I wasn't caring about them, then, or myself."

Kerry: *"At night my brother and sister would call to talk to me. . . . I didn't want to speak to them. I wasn't caring about them, then, or myself."*

Finally Kerry stayed at a friend's house for such a long time that her mother threatened to call the police if she didn't return home. "I gave in and even went back to school. But four days later I snapped when a friend got me high on what was supposed to be pot and wasn't. From that drug I got such a bad reaction—my body went out of control. Every part of me was shivering and shaking. My friends tried to keep me warm by piling sweaters and coats on top of me, but nothing worked. I was so freaked out that I didn't know how to get home.

"The next day I had in-school suspension. That night my mother told me she had made an appointment for me to be interviewed at another psychiatric hospital. This one had a program for teenage drug and alcohol abusers. Finally, she had put things together and realized that drugs were causing my mood swings. But my mother also felt I had other serious problems as well: depression and my reaction to the divorce. That's why she thought I needed to be hospitalized.

"After the hospital evaluated me, they said I had an addictive personality. By then I knew I was an addict, so I had no trouble signing myself in as one. Anyhow, if I didn't admit I was addicted, I'd really have been worse off."

By the spring of his senior year, Rob was so lonely boarding at school that he asked his parents if he could live at home. "They said no, so I went to classes in the day and spent my nights on the streets. I'd sleep in my car, which I moved to a different spot every evening. After three weeks my parents gave in.

"That fall I started college. With my high SAT scores, I had been accepted to a good school. I thought that by being in a new environment, I could change my life. But the first day at college, I got high and ended up in a fight where I got a black eye. All the while I had been so sure I could kick my drug habit whenever I wanted to.

"When I was at college I'd travel twelve hours straight on an overnight bus to buy cocaine in the city. The next morning I'd take another bus back to school. Then I'd sell the drugs to the guys, which gave me money to buy more for myself. And as the supplier, I felt accepted. Yet, after a night of hard partying with loads of people, five A.M. would come, and there I'd be, the only one up. I'd sit with whatever drugs I had left, feeling so alone.

"By now my body was a wreck from all the alcohol and drugs. Every morning I'd wake up hungover and stay that way until I got drunk and did drugs again later in the day. It no longer mattered that my hair and clothes were a mess. I was feeling bad and empty. Every minute I was by myself, I thought, 'Who can I call?' "

As soon as Pat was in Florida with his great-grandmother, he found the drug crowd and started hanging out with them. "I wanted friends so badly, yet I didn't know how to go about making them. I'd drink a lot and be the funny man, thinking then everybody liked me. But too much alcohol also made me violent. Before you knew it, I'd be into fights. One time I beat up my best friend because he criticized how I rolled a joint.

"More than anything, I didn't want people finding out too much about my life. When they tried to get near me, I'd push them away. By acting the tough guy, I thought I was copying my father, who would get high, fight, and go to jail.

"Finally my great-grandmother couldn't handle me anymore and sent me back to my grandmother. I was in seventh grade and had missed so much school. That year the school tested me and found out that I only could read on a first-grade level.

"Meanwhile, the high school drug counselor got me into his group program. Bob had known my mother when she went to high school and remembered she was on drugs, so he figured I must be, too. At those meetings, Bob tried to get me to talk, but I wouldn't cooperate. I kept telling him that he could never understand my life and should stop trying to lead it. I didn't want his help nor anyone else's.

"When the public school I was in felt I was too much of a behavior problem, they sent me to an alternative school that was the last place I could go to before I was out of the system. There I met kids who were worse than any I had ever hung out with before. With them I started taking angel dust, which made me think I was in a world where everyone was smiling. I'd walk down the street feeling great, especially now that I had a lot of money in my pocket from dealing cocaine.

"But the drugs would wear off, and I'd feel awful again, wanting to die. To numb myself, I'd smoke and smoke pot, till I passed out.

"That year my grandmother became very sick with cancer. She was the only person in the world who had been sincerely interested in me, but I didn't appreciate her at the time. Two years before she got sick, she had arranged to get me into a residential drug treatment center covered by her insurance. When I refused to go, she had her friend's two huge sons physically take me there. I hated my grandmother for doing this. When the center took me off drugs I went into a rage. Six months later I was discharged, and on the first day out of treatment, I got high on dust. I had no interest in being helped.

"Now that she had cancer, my grandmother's dying wish was that I get straight. This time she brought me to an out-patient drug treatment center and drove me there six mornings a week, picking me up at the end of the day. She was determined to do everything in her power so I could get my life together. But I kept screwing up.

"When she died a year later, I was so angry. I felt, again, somebody had left me.

"Right before my grandmother died, I moved in with my father, who was back on heroin. My drug habit, too, was worse than ever. I sold everything I owned to support it—even my jacket. By now I was spending all my time on the street, getting high, while my sisters were living upstate with our mother, who had just married the boyfriend who had abused all of us.

"At this time, crack was really big, and I couldn't get enough of it. Once when I was making a deal, some guys near me started shooting. I was so scared. At that moment I just wanted someone to hold me and tell me everything would be okay. I felt like a little, lost child.

"Later on, though, I told the story of the shooting to my friends and said the whole shoot-out was no big deal."

Whenever Cindy drank a lot, she'd have blackouts where she'd lose control of her bladder and urinate in her pants. From all the cocaine she took, she also imagined hearing and seeing things that didn't exist. "In a room full of people, I'd suddenly get quiet and say, 'Shh, what's that?' Each sound made me suspicious. I literally walked with my back against the wall, that's how afraid I was that someone might hurt me.

"Even so, I still kept going into tough neighborhoods to get drugs. One night the guy I was with robbed a store. When the police found us, I was higher than a kite. My hands were shaking, and my mouth was so dry from all the cocaine I had just snorted that I couldn't even say my name. When they brought me to the police station, I saw flakes of coke on the walls and on uniforms.

"The police didn't find drugs on me, so I was released. But realizing I might have gone to jail frightened me. It made me hate myself more than ever.

"Meanwhile, my sister, Liz, saw what was happening and told me I was turning into a waste. As I was heavy into drugs, she was going to college full-time, working as a waitress to pay her tuition.

"Although I too had hopes of graduating from high school, I kept allowing drugs to get in the way. Every morning I'd plan to go to classes, but before my eyes were even open, somebody would be at my door tempting me. It didn't take me more than a second to rush out of the house and get high with them. I wouldn't date or go to dances or to the football games. Only drugs were on my mind.

"By this time my mother suspected I was taking drugs, but she thought drugs were just a phase with me. Whenever I was hungover, she'd call the school or my job, giving some excuse why I couldn't be there.

"After that incident with the police, though, I started thinking more about my life. I saw that so much of it was spent hanging around grungy people who'd turn me on, then leave me alone to do their dealing. I felt so empty. Even cocaine didn't help. At seventeen, I was a rag doll who had bottomed out.

"Finally I got fed up living this way. One morning I got up real early and went straight to the drug counselor's office in school. I hadn't showered, and

I was wearing two different-colored socks. 'Cocaine is destroying me,' I said to the counselor. 'I need help.'

"The counselor looked at me without saying a word, waiting to hear what I wanted to do next. It was smart of him not to try to push anything down my throat. I told him I wanted to go to a residential drug treatment center where a friend of mine had been, and the counselor thought it was a good idea. But first he said we had to call my mother. Although I knew she had an idea I was on cocaine, from her comments about my constant runny nose and wads of tissues she found under my pillow, I still hated having it brought into the open. But I had no choice.

"Within minutes my mother and Liz were at the school. In front of them both, I said I was a drug addict. Never in my life had I felt so disgusting. When my mother started crying, I didn't react, although I hated people getting emotional. I had reached the end of the line and was like the walking dead."

While pot was John's drug of choice, he used

more powerful drugs, too, including
of all the different drugs he took, Ju
sleep at night. The drugs also affected hi:
"A few hours after I'd eat dinner, I couldn
what I had had.

"In school I barely passed anything. I'd sit in class, looking like a dirt bag, drawing strange designs while everybody else participated. The teachers left me alone 'cause they were convinced that I was a good kid who had emotional problems. Not one of them ever talked to me about drugs. And if any had, or if they'd asked me if I was addicted, I would have answered, 'Nah,' because that's what I believed.

"At this time I tried as much as possible to keep away from my family, especially my father. When I'd come home, I'd go right to my bedroom and close the door. Like a hermit, I'd stay there for hours, listening to heavy metal. I liked that kind of music because I thought those groups could understand my violent feelings.

"Although my mother saw how I was acting, she never said a word. Today she tells me that she thought my problems were more emotional than having to do with drugs. Even if she had tried to talk to me then, I would have closed my ears. I was like a wall that couldn't hear a thing.

"I lied or kept things so hidden that my therapist too had no way of knowing how I felt. Still, I wish he could have figured out what was going on, because in the end, I was left all alone in my own hazy world.

"One hot summer day while I was with friends, cruising around in a pickup truck, I had a bad reaction from drinking warm whiskey and smoking hash. I told the guys I felt real sick and wanted to be let out. Behind the Seven-Eleven store, I found a secluded spot where I couldn't stop throwing up, and I had such horrible stomach pains. For four and a half hours I lay in the dirt, drooling all over myself. I was so embarrassed that someone might see me. Never have I felt so alone in my life. It was sheer hell.

"After this happened I used drugs and alcohol for another year. Every morning I'd wake up and tell myself, 'No more pot. No more drinking. No more lying,' thinking this would be the day when my life would change. But it never happened.

"By this time my father had been in AA for two years. Although he had given up drinking, he still hit me. Now I thought I deserved the beatings, because I felt like such a bad person, who even did things like smashing kids' pumpkins on Halloween just to be one of the guys.

"From what he learned in AA, my father had a good idea I was addicted, too. However, he didn't pay attention to my brother's drinking, because my brother was functioning well in college and also had a job.

"One day both of my parents told me that if I wanted to continue living with them, I had to take urine tests to make sure I wasn't on drugs. I had no idea what they were seeing, since I thought I had hidden my drug problem so well.

"Then I noticed books on drugs around the house and wondered what it was all about. I knew I had a lot of pain and needed to get stoned, but I never realized I was an addict.

"When I failed one of the tests, my parents gave me a choice. They said I could either go to in-patient or out-patient rehab. Naturally, I chose out-patient. Together, my parents brought me to the treatment center. I had just turned sixteen."

By the time Jeff was eighteen, he had quit school and was seriously addicted to crack. The drug made him so violent that in rages he would destroy anything around. "My parents were now back together again, in the same house, and my father especially didn't want me to live with them. He knew my cousin was on drugs, and from my reddened eyes and sniffing, he suspected I was, too.

"To protect himself and the rest of the family from me, he changed the locks on the doors and put alarms on every window. I had nowhere to go. In desperation, I'd manipulate my mother to let me in.

"That same year my girlfriend became pregnant, so we got our own apartment. She worked as a page for a law firm and wasn't on drugs, but she knew I was. At night when I'd come in with wide-open eyes, she'd say, 'You high again?' With all this, I still managed to be at my job at a gas station.

"Not long after our son, Jeff Jr., was born, my girlfriend became pregnant again. This time we had a girl, whom we named Hope. By then my drug problem was worse than ever. The money I got from my job and dealing wasn't nearly enough to pay for the crack I needed. After I had sold or pawned all of my jewelry, I started taking things from the house, like the stereo. If I couldn't find anything to sell, I'd wreck the place. When it came to drugs, everyone watch out!

"One day when I came home, I found that my girlfriend had moved out, taking the children with her. She didn't even leave a note telling me where she had gone. Never was I so alone in my life. I was on the verge of flipping out. If I didn't get help, I knew I'd go crazy. That night I called my mother and told her I wanted to come home."

The longer Donna was on drugs, the tougher she acted. "In my black leather jacket and mini skirt, I looked like I invited trouble. When I was fifteen I got into Satanism, like everybody else in my crowd. I didn't really believe in Satan, but I followed the group when they said prayers to him. One night, while drinking and tripping out on mescaline, I had a fight with a girl. As I was beating her up, everyone behind me shouted, 'Burn her. Burn her.' So I said, 'Okay.' Luckily, I stopped in time. It was as if something suddenly clicked in my head and said, 'Donna, you're not a violent person.' Even after that incident, though, I didn't stop doing drugs.

"During the time I was on drugs, I went to a number of funerals for friends. Some died from overdosing; others had committed suicide. Two girlfriends, while high on drugs, were killed in a car accident. After each funeral, a group of us would walk out together, depressed. Immediately someone would say, 'Can you pass the mirror.' Then we'd all do some lines.

"More than once I considered quitting drugs, but then in school I'd see my friends, and in a poof, I'd start smoking a joint with them. Afterward, I'd say, 'Donna, you did it again, didn't you?'

"On the Christmas Eve I was sixteen I went out drinking with friends. When I came in that night, my mother told me to pack my bags and leave. I remember going up to my room to get my things, but then I blacked out. To this day I don't recall what happened next, or if my sister, Laura, was in the house to witness it. But the next morning when I awoke, my room was trashed. Glass from my picture frames was all over the place, and I was the one who had wrecked everything.

"For the first time I saw how I was destroying myself. Deep down I wanted to make it, but I knew that by living at home and hanging out with the drug crowd, I'd never have a chance. So I decided to make a complete break."

CHAPTER 5

WANTING TO GET BETTER

ON CHRISTMAS DAY Donna called her aunt to see if she could move in with her and her family. A few weeks before, Donna, with her aunt and mother, had talked about this possibility. "Aunt Roseanne was the only person in the family whom I respected. Although she had two kids almost my age, she took me in, knowing I was on drugs. Her home was the first stable one I experienced.

"As soon as I was settled there, my mother found me a therapist. In the beginning I didn't trust the therapist, so I spent the hour listening to her talk. But with time I began to open up and describe the life I had led. Looking back, she turned out to be one of the best people I ever met. I stayed with her for a year.

"Along with therapy, I also had the support of my friend Marci, whom I had known since ninth grade. Marci too was getting off drugs. Particularly then, her friendship was invaluable to me. Whenever I'd want to smoke a joint, she'd talk me out of it. Or if I wanted to hang out with the drug crowd, she'd suggest we go for a hike or to the movies. Aunt Roseanne helped, too. She pinned a calendar on the wall and had me mark the days I didn't drink or take drugs. Sometimes a week would go by when I'd be clean. I'd say, 'Oh, wow! Okay!'

"Meanwhile, when I moved I had to change schools and make new friends. Immediately I looked for kids who were on drugs 'cause those were the kind of people I was used to. But I was determined not to do drugs with them and told the group right away. When they heard that I was quitting, they said they'd support me. Every time they passed around joints, I was automatically skipped. To this day I'm not sure why they went out of their way for me. Most drug groups won't accept newcomers, let alone those who don't get high with them.

Donna: *"In the beginning I'd . . . call my mother, begging her to let me come home. Although I was so angry with her . . . I was lonely without her there."*

"Even with all the people behind me, I still had it hard. In the beginning I'd have withdrawal fits and would call my mother, begging her to let me come home. Although I was so angry with her, she was still the parent I had always lived with, and I was lonely without her there. But she said I had to stay at my aunt's, knowing if I came back it wouldn't be good for either of us. Instead, we spoke on the phone every night, and once a week she and Laura visited. In the beginning, my mother and I argued when we were together, but the more therapy I had, the better we did.

"One thing that really bothered me was that I had left my sister alone. At first, I had been only thinking about myself, but later on I wanted her at Aunt Roseanne's with me. Yet I realized it wouldn't work.

"To complicate matters, I started dating a guy who turned out to be an addict, too, although I didn't know this when we met. Soon we ended up doing cocaine whenever we were together. One night he didn't bring any and said that the two of us had to quit. Initially I was angry with him, but then, with his family's support, I finally stopped. That year I was in eleventh grade. When I got my report card, I had made the honor roll."

After living with her aunt and uncle for a year, Donna moved into her own apartment. She was only seventeen years old. "For a while I liked living with Aunt Roseanne, but as time passed, I felt out of place and closed in. Once I got off drugs, I thought I needed to get totally away from the family. When I told the school social worker about my problem, she wrote a letter for me so I could get legal rights to live alone. She also helped me find an apartment, which my father paid for as part of child support.

"As much as I had wanted to be on my own, it also made me anxious. Soon I went back to smoking pot. When I'd get to school and was asked to read aloud, the words in the book seemed all jumbled. I couldn't tell what language they were in. Now I saw I couldn't deal with drugs anymore. After a month I gave up pot, even though I still had strong urges for it. Sometimes I'd be all alone in my room, going out of my mind for a joint. I'd have this conversation with myself where I'd say, 'Now Donna, if you want a joint, you can get one. Should you, though?' Sweating as I rocked back and forth, I would finally talk myself out of getting high.

"When I turned eighteen I started college, and for almost the whole school year, I stayed away from drugs. I'd be with a bunch of girls who'd be smoking pot, but I wouldn't touch any. Right after I finished finals though, I decided to smoke a joint with a friend. The next morning I woke up feeling spaced out. My head was so heavy that I couldn't lift it off the pillow. I decided that taking pot had definitely not been worth it.

"Later on that day I got real upset when I thought about what I had done. I was sure I had thrown everything away for one joint. After having done so well, I was mad that I had messed up. When I confided in a friend, she told me not to feel guilty, but she added that I shouldn't take a joint again. Since that time I've not been tempted. It's been over a year."

The year Pat turned sixteen, he began to steal to

get drug money. One night he and his friend were arrested for taking a car. "As the policeman handcuffed me, I thought, now I'll go to jail, just like my father. But suddenly I knew I didn't want his kind of life. I almost started crying, not believing what was happening to me!

"Both my parents were with me in court when the judge asked me to decide whether I wanted to spend a minimum of seven years in prison or go into drug treatment. I chose rehab, knowing this was my last chance to get straightened out. The minute we left the courthouse, my father beat me up.

"Two weeks later, with the parole office at my side, I was back at the same drug treatment center my grandmother had brought me to before she died. Since I had no money to make payments, there was no charge.

"That first week in treatment I drank a lot and smoked joints. But after that I went straight, 'cause every time my rehab leader suspected I might get high, she threatened to call my probation officer. She knew my greatest fear was going to jail.

Pat: *"I saw I had it in me to change."*

"Now I've been in the program for over two years, and all that time I've managed to stay sober. But it hasn't been easy. Especially in the beginning, I'd get fed up with things and think about quitting treatment. Whenever that happened, people in rehab would remind me about my past and ask if I wanted to go back to my old life. That meant ending up like my father, on heroin, with a gun pointed to my head. Finally I wanted to live, and with each day, I saw I had it in me to change."

One night in family counseling, Danielle came into the therapist's office stoned. Immediately everyone knew what was going on. "Right then and there, the therapist told my parents to take me to the National Council on Alcohol and Drugs. People at the council recommended I go into residential treatment, and they suggested a place halfway across the country. By now I hated my life, but I didn't want to be sent away. I felt my parents were pointing the finger at *me* again, by making *me* leave, while Jennifer was allowed to stay home. Today my mother says she hadn't realized my sister was as deeply into drugs as I. But even staying at home scared Jennifer. While I was in treatment, she stopped doing drugs, cold turkey, on her own.

"The month and a half I was away, I had no drugs or even a cigarette. And when I came home, I didn't do drugs either. But I went right back to my old friends, who were getting high.

"Then my parents sent me to a boarding school, thinking maybe there I'd make new friends and get on track. But things didn't work out the way they planned. At the school I became very depressed, because I felt my parents had pushed me out of the house and didn't want me anymore. Despite all the fighting that went on between my mother and me, I still missed her. One night I tried to kill myself. When I called my parents and told them I had taken an overdose of pills, they were able to get someone to bring me to a hospital. A few days later my parents said I could come home to live. The only provision was that I had to be a full-time outpatient in a drug rehabilitation center.

"Since I no longer took drugs, I couldn't understand why I needed *any* treatment. But my mother, who had grown up in an alcoholic family, felt differently. She knew how serious addiction can be. After talking to the family therapist, she and my father said I had no choice but to go into rehab.

"With rehabilitation treatment came new limits. Not only did I now have to follow my mother's rules, I had to do things in a certain way at the treatment center. In the beginning I hated that. *I* wanted to be in charge! Every time the leader in rehab told me something I didn't like, I'd get angry and run out of the door. Yet I always came back because the leader kept in close contact with my mother.

"For the first nine months I was in treatment full-time, taking my classes there. Then I was ready to cut back to two nights a week and return to my public high school.

"By now a lot of the kids I used to hang out with had graduated, and others were in a vocational program somewhere else. Although my friend Judy was still around, she had given up drugs when her boyfriend went into treatment. So I didn't have to worry about being pressured to do drugs with the old crowd.

"Besides, I had new friends from the treatment center, and they turned out to be the best people I ever met in my whole life. One was a year younger than me and another was six years older. In rehab, a friend's age doesn't matter. After sharing so much pain, you become real close. Today, whenever I do something these friends think might hurt me, they come right out and let me know. They are the most amazing people. I love them because they care so much."

When John started group counseling at the drug and alcohol treatment center, he still drank even though he knew it was against the rules. "To me life was a game where everybody lied to each other. So why would I be honest to the group? The only reason I told them about my pot slips is because I had stopped doing drugs.

"But in treatment there was one person I trusted, and that was my individual counselor. As soon as we met I liked her, because she didn't bully me.

One day I told her I was still drinking, and without threatening to ship me off, she said matter-of-factly that I had to stop and go to AA. By then I was already in rehab three days a week, spending four to five hours at a time there.

"Meanwhile, I kept hanging out with my old buddies, and I was still shoplifting. But I had a new friend—at the center—and he was sober. After knowing each other about two months, he invited me to his house. We had so much fun without getting wasted. Besides this friend, I was also getting along with Jim, my group leader. Things were looking up.

"One night I decided to go to AA to hear Jim speak. There a member approached me and asked if I'd like to sign up. I said, 'Not today. I'm going on vacation.' It was the July fourth weekend, and I was leaving to visit my half sister and her husband. I knew that my brother-in-law drank and took drugs, and I was torn about what I should do while I was at their house. As I unpacked my suitcase, I told myself I could handle one beer at dinner. I was sure I could control that.

"Then as we watched TV, my brother-in-law offered me another beer, and I took it. I also drank some of his homemade wine. By the end of the weekend I had even gotten stoned with him, breaking all my promises to myself. Instead of going home that Sunday, I stayed the rest of the week. On one of the nights there my brother-in-law's friend came by with coke. I had never done coke before, so my brother-in-law told me to watch how he and his friend got on it. Then he said, 'Here John, I saved you a line.' As I started to snort, I saw my reflection in the mirror, and I felt horrible. But not horrible enough to stop. I kept snorting away, and afterward, I drank and drank until I felt nothing.

"That Sunday when my father picked me up to take me home, I said to him in the car, 'You guys were right. I'm addicted.' It was the first time I was ever honest with him or myself.

"The next day I told the group at the treatment center that I had gotten wasted and that I had had enough of that kind of life. Not long after I went back to AA and found the guy who had asked me to join. 'Sign me up,' I said to him, 'and you be my sponsor.' From that moment I never got drunk or stoned again. It's almost two years that I've been clean.

"I'd like to say that at this point everything ended happily ever after. But truthfully, I did a lot of rebelling when I first went into AA. I argued with everybody who disagreed with me and I was so arrogant. I thought I knew it all.

"Then one day my sponsor and I drove to Tennessee to attend a weekend international conference for young people held by AA. At that meeting I really changed. There I met kids my age, who were so honest. For the first time I shared things about myself that I had sworn never to tell anyone. This group knew how I was feeling because they had gone through similar experiences. They helped me understand that I didn't need to be perfect to be accepted. With time I got back my sense of humor and also started drawing and writing poetry again. But more important, I stopped running away from my problems."

*   *   *

Now that Jeff was back living with his parents, his mother saw what terrible shape he was in. "I told my mother a little about the life I had been leading and said I no longer wanted it anymore. I hated the way I was: a manipulative, sneaky person, who lied all the time.

"A few weeks before my girlfriend moved out with the kids, I had made an appointment at the drug rehab center near the house. But I didn't show up for the date. Nor was I there for the next appointment. My girlfriend kept saying to me, 'You call, but you ain't gonna do nothing.' It was true.

"Now another appointment was coming up that I had made just before I had come home. I told my mother about it, and I said to her, 'Take me there!' She agreed. My mother brought her twenty-year-old son—the father of two kids—in for drug treatment."

During his first week in rehab Jeff would leave the treatment center at the end of the day, and then get high. In five days he had smoked close to a hundred vials of crack. "That Saturday I didn't show up for rehab at all, but instead went back to my old apartment, where I found a stash of crack. I never left the house that day. I thought, this is going to be my last time smoking.

"From all the crack, I started hallucinating and imagined that a snake was crawling up my leg. Without thinking, I ripped off my pants while holding a lit match and burned myself so badly. When I look at the scar today, I'm reminded of the life I used to lead.

"Meanwhile, the incident left me petrified. So I called my mother to come and get me. She and my father were so furious with what I was doing that they threatened to turn me out again. Finally I made up my mind that I was going to stop doing drugs. That Monday I went back to rehab and started the program. I've been in it for the past eight months.

"Once I decided to plunge myself into treatment, I went full force. Whatever I was told to do, I followed. I wanted to get better fast. My biggest problem was not having enough patience. I had to get things done *now*. It was as if I was in a fifty-five-mile-an-hour speed zone, going at seventy-five.

Two months after being in rehab, I had a relapse.

"This really scared me. I thought I was going to be like my big brother at the center, who'd go three months straight, mess up, then start over and then over again. When the counselors saw how discouraged I was, they helped me. Without screaming or pointing a finger, they showed me which attitudes of mine had to be changed. It wasn't easy accepting their suggestions. But I knew that they cared.

"Because of the neighborhood where I live, it's especially hard for me to keep away from drugs. Every time I go to the store, I pass drug dealers who remember that I used to get high. They say to me, 'Yo, what's up?' I just walk on. Sometimes, though, I want to smoke crack or drink a beer, and I talk about that in rehab. Getting out those feelings is much better for me than being stoned. That's for sure!"

Although Kerry voluntarily entered the psychiatric hospital, she went in with the attitude that she knew everything. "At first I was real snotty, thinking I could tell the staff something about hospitals. Whenever anybody tried to help me, I wouldn't give them the time of day. It didn't matter if I liked the person or not.

"Finally a staff member ran out of patience and said right to my face what she thought of me. It wasn't pretty, but she was honest. From then on, she became a good friend. I'll never forget her.

"Another staff person at the hospital was like a mommy figure. When everyone was in bed, she'd come into the rooms and hug each of us good-night. That felt so good.

"From the beginning I met a couple of times a week with a private therapist in the hospital. She was young and understood me. Of all people, I've been most honest with her. I still meet with her once a week. While at the hospital, I also went to NA [Narcotics Anonymous], but mostly I talked about my drug problem in psychological counseling.

"By now, of course, my family knew I had been on drugs. Yet I still had trouble admitting my past to them. If I wanted them to trust me, the secrets had to come out.

"As part of the hospital program, MFG [multiple family group] is held, where the addicted kid tells everyone the truth while being video-taped. One day it was my turn to speak. I was so nervous having my parents, sister, and brother there. With one hand I clutched my sister, who sat on my lap, while with the other I tightly held onto my friend. Finally I said aloud, 'I did drugs, and I drank a lot.' My mother started crying."

After Rob had completed his second semester at college, he came home for a vacation break. By now his parents, with the help of a therapist, knew he was addicted. One morning, without saying a word, his mother and father brought him to an out-patient treatment center. "As we drove along the avenue where the center was, I realized what was up, but I didn't care. To me, rehab was just another one of those deals that I was sure wouldn't work out. Later in the car, after my interview, I screamed and cursed my parents, telling them they couldn't stop me from drinking and taking drugs. They said, 'Yes we can.' I had no idea what they meant. To get them off my back, I decided to stay in rehab for two months, then go back to my old life at college.

"When I went to the first meeting at the treatment center, I expected the other people in the program to be completely different from me. After all, I wasn't your standard drug addict with alcoholism, divorce, or abuse in my background. But then I listened to the kids there talk, and I saw I had a lot more in common with them than I'd imagined. Hearing them describe how badly they felt about themselves and what they did to get others to like them made me realize we shared similar problems. That night and the next day, I didn't drink or get high.

"On Saturday morning I went back to the center for another meeting. This one was with people who were in the program full-time. They knew a lot about themselves and why they had gotten into drugs. And they were very honest with one another. If someone disagreed with another person, he said right out how he felt. I had never heard people be so up front. It made me nervous. Still, I went back to the center the following Monday night. After a week of being in the program, I completely stopped drinking and doing drugs. It wasn't even a conscious thing. I quit, just like that!"

As soon as Rob had entered the treatment program, he cut himself off from whatever he used to do. "The first thing I did was get a job picking up garbage for the village. I worked from five in the morning till eleven A.M., then rushed home to shower and change my clothes so I'd be ready for my other job in the city, where I wrote programs for computers. Two nights a week and all day Saturday, I went to rehab. With these long hours I had little time to socialize. Anyhow, there were no college kids around for me to hang out and get high with.

"But one day, when I had been in treatment for a few months, a girl I knew invited me to a pool party. I stopped by to see what it was like and found that everyone there was drinking. After an hour I left—not having touched a thing. From that moment on I felt like I had removed myself from my old life.

"Today I realize that stopping drugs was pretty easy compared to talking about my feelings. I was so used to stuffing everything inside that it scared me to tell anyone how I felt. When I'd be in group meetings, I'd mostly stay quiet and keep to myself.

"After I'd been in treatment a few months, I took part in an extended group session where about ten of us stayed up all night, talking about serious issues. It made me feel very close to everyone, and for the first time, I let my defenses down, crying, without feeling embarrassed.

"That whole experience was a turning point for me. From then on I started being honest with myself and my parents, too. Little by little, I told my parents about my life. The closer we became, the more I saw they had wanted the same things for me that I wanted for myself—to succeed and be happy.

"Now it's more than three years that I've been off drugs and alcohol. I haven't had a single relapse, although I admit there are moments when I get tempted, like when I see a beer advertisement. While I haven't had a drink in so long, I still can almost taste the stuff by just looking at the picture. Luckily I don't get these urges very often. Yet I have a real fear about using alcohol again. So when I go alone on a business trip, I make sure I'm extra careful."

Although Cindy wanted to go in for drug rehabilitation right after she had talked to the counselor at school, she had to wait the entire weekend until there was a free bed for her. "Suddenly I began to have second thoughts about quitting drugs. That Saturday and Sunday I smoked pot like I never had done before. I kept thinking that this might be it! After I partied with the crowd, I went to my dad's and got high with him.

"That Monday morning when my mother woke me up, she had me packed and ready to go. But I took my time, smoking a joint before I went into the car. Then my mother and stepfather drove me to the rehab center, which was covered by my dad's insurance.

"For me the best part about being in residential treatment was that I could get away from my neighborhood and my drug friends. With my bad reputation at home, there was no way I could make it.

At least now I had a chance to break away. But rehab wasn't easy.

"Especially in the beginning, I couldn't get used to the discipline and the rules. I never had had to deal with those kinds of things before. At the treatment center I had to get up at six in the morning and go to bed at ten. It took me time to adjust, but once I did, I kind of liked having limits.

"Meanwhile, every Sunday, my mother and sister came to see me, and sometimes my father visited, too. Liz and Mom took part in the family counseling program at the center, but my father had no interest.

"In rehab a miracle happened. For the first time I started listening to people. As kids talked about how happy they were to be off drugs, I'd sit with my eyes glued to them, thinking they were gods. When they talked about living, I really tuned in. I wanted to live so badly.

"What surprised me is that these people were my age and like me in so many ways—their feelings, their insecurities, their family problems. They weren't the skid-row type I had expected. Still, it took me a while to open up with them. I didn't want to deal with all the garbage from my past. And I had such a low opinion of myself. When I came into treatment, I had no goals, no fantasies, no ambition. Other than softball, I didn't have any interests or hobbies. I was like an old lady without hope.

"After being at the residential treatment center for fifty days, I moved back home. For the next three months I went to out-patient counseling at the same center. During that time I also joined Alcoholics Anonymous, going to meetings seven days a week. Plus I enrolled in another treatment center for group and individual counseling and went there three times a week. Every minute of my life was occupied with treatment, school, and my job at Carvel's. It was a rough period, but I managed to get through it. At least my mother and stepfather weren't drinking anymore, which helped a lot. They stopped when I went into treatment, and they went to a few rehab meetings, too.

"My mother, in particular, realized how important my recovery was. She'd keep reminding me that it came first before anything else. When I had to be at AA or a meeting at the center and couldn't finish my homework, she'd say, 'You can always take the course again.'

"With all the support I was getting, I still was afraid I wouldn't know how to handle my problems. For so long I had relied on drugs and alcohol to get me through each hassle. In the past if a boyfriend broke up with me, I'd say, 'So what!' Then I'd take a joint or snort some coke to feel better. Now if I was going to be sober, I'd have to deal with my feelings. I told my group in treatment how scary this was, and they understood. Nobody pretended it would be easy.

"Meanwhile, I was so lonely and felt like the new creepy kid in the neighborhood. In school I'd bury my face in a book to avoid my old crowd. At first it was hard to break away from them. They had been such a big part of my life.

"Lucikly, my mother was smart enough to talk to my teachers and explain what was going on, and the teachers were very supportive. They complimented me when I looked good or gave the right answers in class. But when they didn't call on me,

I'd start to cry. My emotions then were all over the place.

"Thank goodness I had an AA sponsor I easily could get in touch with. And I could talk to my counselor at the rehab center. So many people were there to show me how to put one foot in front of the other."

CHAPTER 6

LIVING DRUG FREE

AT THE TREATMENT CENTER Cindy learned how to have fun without the help of drugs or alcohol. "I never laughed so hard in my life as with the kids there. We had such a good time together—playing volleyball, going sleigh riding, camping out. For the first time I was acting like a kid.

"Now that I was sober and finding out more about myself, I could see my father more clearly. One night in group therapy I cried as I told everyone that he was killing himself with crack. 'My father is dying before my eyes,' I sobbed. The group listened as I poured out my feelings. They understood.

"After a year at the center, I moved from group counseling to individual sessions. The last day I met with the group, they gave me a coin as a gift. On one side were praying hands, while the other had the words *One day at a time*. I've attached that coin to my key chain, which I always carry around.

"A few months ago I celebrated my third anniversary in sobriety. To mark that milestone, my group leader in Alcoholics Anonymous praised me at a meeting. When he talked about my involvement in AA and said that I was a sensitive, caring person and a powerful example, my eyes filled with tears.

"Today I'm living with a girlfriend, and I work as a secretary for an agency that helps people who have serious personal problems. Before I could get this job, though, I needed special clerical training as well as tutoring in basic elementary subjects.

"When I graduated high school, I was so uneducated that I didn't know how to read a newspaper or what the seven continents were. At seventeen I drove a car but couldn't understand a road map. To this day I've not caught up, so I go for tutoring once a week. At the moment we're working on measurements.

"I wish I could go to college, one day, so I can teach physical education on the high-school level. But because of all the work I have to do on myself, and all the schooling I've missed, I may never get to that point. That makes me sad. I keep thinking, what a person I could have been if I hadn't gotten into drugging and drinking!

"Meanwhile, I'm doing whatever I can so my life will be better. To keep in shape, I take aerobics and I play softball. Once a week I meet with my counselor at the treatment center, and two or three times a week I go to AA. In my mind, AA comes before anything else. I know I'll need it forever because I'm an alcoholic.

"Since I've been off drugs, I get along better with my mother, and I've also become much closer to my sister. Today Liz is married and has two children, and I'm the godmother of her son, who's two and a half. On weekends I take him apple picking, or we play miniature golf. I know my sister trusts me, because otherwise I wouldn't get to have her kids alone.

"Although Liz never did drugs or alcohol, my

sister and I share many of the same feelings and worries since we're both children of alcoholics. Whenever we get together we talk about our family problems.

"At the moment one of the biggest issues I'm dealing with is my father. Although he stopped doing drugs and drinking two years ago when he went to jail, I still can't forget what he's done to me. He never acted like a parent, but treated me instead like another drug buddy. This is very hard for me to deal with, so I got to a therapist who's helping me sort out things.

"At least with alcohol and drugs out of the picture, I can concentrate on improving my own life. I can't believe how much I have changed in the past three and a half years. If I'm angry with people, I let them know why. If I'm sad, I'm not ashamed to cry in front of them. Because I've become more honest with my feelings, my friends feel comfortable being open with me, too.

"A short while back I went on a camping trip with my best girlfriend. Four years ago I never would have even considered leaving my town, except to buy drugs. And I wouldn't have dreamed of having fun without a guy at my side. Today I jump at the chance to have different experiences. It makes me feel so much freer."

After not seeing his two children for a while, Jeff finally decided he was ready to visit them. Somebody Jeff knew was able to get word to his girlfriend and tell her that Jeff was sober. "This past weekend I took the kids to the park. Off drugs, I finally could enjoy them. They're so beautiful to watch. At one point Jeff Jr., who's two and a half, came to me crying 'cause a little kid hit him. A year ago I would have pushed him away and said, 'Go beat him up!' Instead, I held him tightly and told him it's okay for boys to cry. I used to think fighting made you a man, but today I realize how important it is for kids to let out their feelings. Maybe if they learn to cry early on, they won't escape into beer or drugs when they're older.

"I can't believe how much I've changed in such a short time. In rehab I took a test for my General Equivalency High School Diploma and scored so high that I've applied to college. At this moment I'm waiting to see if I get accepted to the school I chose. If I get in, I plan to go to college full-time, taking accounting so I can run my own business. Meanwhile, I'm working at my father's shop. And I'm trying to stay drug free. But because of my family situation, this isn't easy.

"Every night when I come home from the treatment center, I have to face my parents, who continue to drink. Whenever I open the refrigerator, there's beer staring at me from the shelf. This past weekend my father cooked goat stew with wine in it, knowing I won't eat any food that's made with alcohol. Other times he'll drink and say to me, 'Want some?' Then he'll see my angry face and say, 'Oh, I forgot.'

"Recently I asked him and my mother, too, why they don't stop drinking. Each made up an excuse, which reminded me of myself a while back, when I'd find any reason to get high—if I felt bad, if I felt good, if the sun was shining, if it was raining.

"The other night I tried to get my father to quit, but he wasn't interested. I should know that I can't change my parents. I can only work on myself. Still, that night I cried."

When Pat entered the drug treatment program, he barely could read or write, but in rehabilitation they taught him how. Now he can send a letter to someone without being embarrassed. "Nobody can imagine how good that feels. Every time I meet people who talk about giving up school, I try to discourage them by showing them where an education has gotten me.

"After I was in the program for twenty months, my treatment was cut down to two nights a week. That's when I started trade school to learn about the construction and building industry, and I also got a job with a plumber. Two years ago I couldn't have done either, because I had no confidence in myself, and I was always high.

"Today I dream of one day having my own construction company. Even though I can be lazy, if I want something, I go after it. And I want to be successful in business. Since I've quit drugs, I also think more about the future. Finally knowing what a 'normal' family is makes me want to get married and have kids. But that won't happen for a long time because there's a lot of stuff I have to take care of first.

"A few months ago I brought my twin sisters to an in-patient rehab center near where they live with our mother. I thought maybe I could help them get their lives straight, too. But it didn't work out the way I'd planned. They hit each other so much that the center discharged them. Here I thought I could finally save my sisters, but now I see I can't force them to do what they're not ready for. I don't want them to rebel the way I did. As it turns out, I can only take care of myself.

"Another problem I'm struggling with is my father's drinking. I see him a lot, because I live with my grandmother, and he likes to visit his mother. At one point I tried to get close to him and was able to convince him to come to family group meetings with me. But he didn't stay in the program long.

"As for my mother, she wouldn't get involved in my treatment at all. If it was up to her, we'd be smoking joints together.

Pat: *"Today I like who I am."*

"So when it comes down to it, I realize I'm in rehab for myself. Even if I was off probation, I'd still be in the program. It's helped me feel better about myself and recognize what a determined person I am.

"Today I like who I am, but there are still things about me I want to change. Now that I've quit smoking, I'd like to lose weight. And I have to work on controlling my temper. Although I don't hit people anymore, when I get angry I still rage, and the explosions scare me. I used to think I was such a tough person, but now I realize I'm like a sensitive little kid who's had a lot of pain.

"The way I see it, quitting drugs wasn't such a big deal. I had no trouble saying good-bye to drugs and alcohol. But learning about Pat-the-person-behind-the-drugs is another story."

Kerry has been in recovery for nine months. Four of those months she was in the psychiatric hospital. "This past September I started going to a boarding school that is much smaller and more structured than the public school I was in. I have to work harder in this school, and I can't cut classes without expecting to pay for it. Instead of just hanging around at three o'clock, I take part in school activities. Right now I'm cheerleading with my friends at basketball games.

"Even with all this good stuff, I miss the kids from my old school. Some are still on drugs but others are pulling off. I think they got scared when two guys from the group, while high, were killed this past Christmas in a car accident. I know I was very upset when I heard the news. That night I went out and got drunk and smoked pot. It wasn't my first relapse. A few months before I relapsed when my cousin was seriously hurt while driving drunk. What really bothers me is that I had promised myself not to touch alcohol and drugs again, but for some reason, I go back to them whenever things go wrong. At least I have AA, where I can talk about this with the group.

"And I confide in a teacher at school who's also in recovery. Of all people, he's supported me the most these last few months. I really trust him. Every week he takes a group of us to AA meetings.

Kerry, with Arabella, left, and Nina, right: *"I've made new friends at boarding school."*

If I go back to my old high school in the fall, which I'd like to, I'll miss him a lot.

"Although I've made plenty of progress this year, my mother worries because I still hang out with some of my old friends. Even though I've made new friends at boarding school, when I'm home on the weekend, I want to be with my crowd. I miss them. Now that I'm getting my life in order, I want to go back to my old school next year and live at home with my mother. I've asked her about this, and she says she's not yet sure what we'll do.

"At least my mother trusts me more than she used to. This past weekend she let me go to a school dance, realizing that some of the old crowd would be there. I promised her beforehand that I wouldn't get high, and when I came home that night, she saw that I was okay.

"Since my mother and I have a better relation-ship, we have a lot of fun together. On my last school vacation, we went skiing and were hysterical laughing the whole time.

"When I think of all that I've been through, I'm

proud of how things are going today. I like being *me*. Even though I still have a temper, I can control it more. Now I'd like to lose some weight. At school I walk a lot, and at home I do aerobics. Also I try to eat good stuff. This is the first time I've ever taken care of myself.

"For me drinking is the main problem. I realize how much harm it can do, yet whenever I have a big problem, I go back to it. To make it harder, my father is drinking more than ever. When I tell them this in AA, they try to help me, and they encourage me to take it one day at a time.

"As for giving advice to kids about drugs and alcohol, I say not to try either. You never know if you're one who has an addictive personality like I do. Just when you think you're experimenting like everyone else around, you find out too late that you're out of control.

"That's why it's very important for kids to have open relationships with their parents. If they get into trouble, they know where they can get help. But if they lie, they'll get hurt in the end. You can't lie to parents.

"Given the choice, I'd turn back the clock to when I was nine and my parents divorced. From then on I'd do things so differently. Maybe then my life would have been easier."

Today Rob continues with his computer job, which he loves. He's also going to college at night, taking one course a semester. "So far in the classes I've had, I've gotten one B plus and the rest have been As. It's very important to me to finish college and to have a profession. What's funny is that all along my parents wanted this for me and I was rebelling against it.

"If things go well, I plan to marry this girl I've been dating for a while. She's a graduate of the rehab program. Someday I hope we can buy a nice house and raise a family.

"But my major goal is to stay straight. I'd give up my job and even my girlfriend for that. It would be worth not having to go back to the way I used to feel.

"Right now I live with my parents, and the setup seems to be working for all of us. My parents and

I get along much better than we used to. Yet I still feel badly for the trouble and pain I put them through. While my cousins were getting As at Harvard and Princeton, my parents had a son who was out getting high.

"Now that my drug and alcohol problem is no longer a secret, they've told some of our relatives what our life has been like. Except for my grandmother on my father's side, nobody brings up the subject when I see them. But at least it's out in the open. And if anyone asked, I'd have no problem telling them what I did. That's something I'll never deny. It's a part of me.

"In six months I'll be graduating from the rehabilitation program, and I can't believe it. Not that many people make it through. While it was supposed to take a year and a half to complete, I stayed longer, which isn't that unusual.

"Only yesterday I was talking to some friends about how frightening it's going to be without the program's support. I said that I'll probably have to join AA, because I know that I'm going to need treatment for the rest of my life. At this moment

I'm trying to live one day at a time."

When John was on drugs he hated being alone, because then he'd start thinking about how terrible he felt. In recovery for almost two years, he now has no trouble going off by himself. "Near my house is a large farm where I play with the animals or I take walks along the trails. It's so quiet and peaceful there.

"Until recently I didn't realize how much I loved this kind of relaxation. All the years, I tried to be macho like my father, but today I see I'm not at all that type.

"After I had been in treatment for one year, I graduated from the center's program. To celebrate, my group leader surprised me with a piece of cake that had a candle in it. As everybody clapped, I sat squirming in my seat, so embarrassed. Still, I felt good. I had accomplished something very big.

"Today I'm a senior in high school, but I'm taking courses at the local community college because I like their advanced literature and art classes. Besides, I'm treated like a grown-up there. The best part though is that I'm not around burn-outs.

"Since I've been off drugs, I've been able to handle my life so much better. Yesterday at school my car broke down, so I called the garage and arranged for things to be taken care of. Had that happened when I was high, I would have flipped out. But with the help of AA, which I go to every night, I've learned to live one day at a time. I know that if I can stay sober, I'll be fine.

"Today I visit junior high schools, telling kids how drugs almost destroyed my life. It's important for them to hear the truth from others who are close in age to them. Most kids don't realize how dangerous drugs can be. I thought drugs were an entry into manhood, but all they did was lead me to a dead end.

"Now that I don't take drugs, I'm so much happier and laid back. I'm no longer the angry little kid I once was. And I'm doing things I felt I never could before. I've applied to go to a college that specializes in art so I can become an art teacher and devote my time to working with kids. And I'm thinking that maybe one day I'll even get married and have some kids of my own.

"Finally I'm not afraid of the future anymore, nor

do I worry about what the rest of my life will be like. I just try to make the most of each day. If I can stay straight, it will all work out."

One thing that amazes Danielle is that her sister, Jennifer, has been able to stay off drugs without the help of a treatment program. "Some people can do that, and in a way, I envy them. But I've gotten such good stuff from the rehab program that it was worth it.

"What's weird, though, is that I still get a little tempted to go back to my old life. Whenever I see people having a load of fun smoking joints, I want to join them. For the moment I forget how bad things were. Luckily I don't allow myself to give in. I say, 'Danielle, you just can't take a joint and have fun. For you, it becomes a real big mess!'

"As far as getting along with my parents, I'm doing better there, too. Recently I've begun to appreciate what they've done for me during the past two years. Both of my parents have been so supportive, but my mother especially has gone out of her way to make things work. If she hadn't pushed

Danielle: *"Both of my parents have been so supportive, but my mother especially has gone out of her way to make things work."*

me into the rehab program, I wouldn't have gone into treatment. At first I hated her for this, but now I realize she did it because she cared.

"My parents have gone through a lot of pain because of me. It's hurt them to hear about all the things I had done when I was high. But getting everything out in the open brought us closer together.

"Today I spend a lot of time with my mother. Besides driving me to and from the rehab center at all hours and taking me to school, my mother and I hang out with each other. We eat supper together at the diner and go to comedy clubs. Now that I trust my mother, I also confide in her—sometimes about very private issues. In the past I never would have dreamed this could happen.

"Two years have gone by since I've stopped doing drugs, and until now I couldn't find one good thing to say about myself. Now I could go on forever. Finally I like who I am. If other people don't think I'm that great, it's okay.

"In the fall I'll be going to college, where I hope to learn to become an accountant. Before I applied, though, I had to go to summer school to refresh my memory in courses I had missed while on drugs. At present my average is B minus, which is pretty good considering my past. So here's another good thing that's happened in my life. The best, though, is that I'm completely dry. I never had a single relapse in two years—not even a drink of beer!

"I can't say this will always be the case. I have to take it day by day. Right now I don't ever want to pick up another drink or do drugs again. I hope I'll always have the willpower to say no to drugs and alcohol, the way I've already said it so many times. But if for some reason I fall, I'll pick myself up and start again. I know I have the strength and ability to bounce back. I'm a survivor!"

Although Donna has been in recovery for about three years, now and then she goes back to visit her old drug crowd. "I try to think why I'd want to be with these guys, and I've decided it's for the attention I get from them. As soon as they see me, they shout, 'Donna's here!' and give me a hug, which feels good.

"Some of the guys say they're real proud of me, while others resent that I'm not hanging out with them any more. All say how much they love me, but today I know their love isn't the good kind. How can they love me when they don't even love themselves?

"When I think back to the times these guys said they'd protect me no matter what, I realize they weren't thinking about protecting *me*. They would have risked getting killed for any reason, because they didn't value their own lives.

"Maybe the reason I go to see them is to remind myself of how I once was and how far I've come today. Whatever, I'm smart enough not to tell them where I live. If they get into trouble, I don't want any part of it.

"Compared to other twenty-year-olds growing up today, I think I'm very old-fashioned. After running around wild for so many years, I'm much happier leading a calmer life. I go to an all-women's college, where I spend most of my time concentrating on my studies. After I student teach in the morning, I'm either in class or in the library for the rest of the day. Now that I'm not around boys, I no longer worry every minute how I look.

"On weekends at college lots of people party and get drunk, but I don't. I see kids coming back to the dorms, drunk and throwing up, with a hangover in the morning, and I say to myself, 'No thank you.' I can't imagine why they go right out the next week and do it all over again. I can't even stand the taste of alcohol any more. When people come near me smelling of beer, I want to give them a breath spray.

"Lately I've gotten into athletics and feel so much healthier. My roommate teaches me gymnastics every week, and although my body kills after a workout, I'm not quitting. I love sports. Recently I started playing volleyball and tennis, and I'm also swimming. I've wanted to do all this for so long.

"One thing from my drug years that especially bothers me is the influence I've had on my sister. More than anything, I regret having involved Laura with alcohol and drugs. Sometimes I see my old behavior in my sister, and I feel so bad. When I look at the people she hangs out with, I yell, 'Laura, what are you doing? Don't you realize what can happen?' She screams back at me, 'It's my life, anyhow.'

"Laura, who's sixteen, doesn't understand what I'm saying. And I don't want to pressure her, otherwise she might stop confiding in me. Still, I'd like to shout, 'Change! Now!' Yet I realize nobody could have changed me.

"Once in a while Laura stays overnight with me at the dorms. The last time she came, she was all excited because she had gotten a one-hundred on a test. I thought, maybe some of my good habits are rubbing off. I want my sister's life to be easier than mine. I love her so much.

"Since I've been in college, I've made new friends who are the exact opposite from the ones I used to hang out with. All of my friends today are girls who are athletic and preppie. I have so much fun competing in sports with them. Before it was always Donna and a group of guys.

"Except for my roommate, Katie, people at my college have no idea about my past. Even Katie had no clue that I had used drugs until I told her. That makes me feel real good because just two years ago, people still assumed I smoked pot from the tough vibes I gave off.

"Today Katie and Marci, whom I've known for so long, are my best friends. They're the two people I feel most comfortable talking to, and they're both there for me when I feel down. Most of the time, though, I'm all-around happy. Kids who see me say my smile glows.

"Now my highs come from the fantastic grades I've been getting in college. That makes me feel much more satisfied than smoking a joint. For a while I couldn't find anything positive to replace drugs. Then I found it in myself. I realized I had strength and determination, and that I was a sensitive, decent person. Kids need to find things about themselves that they like and stuff they can succeed in. If they get involved in an activity that makes them feel good, they'll be less inclined to smoke pot with a friend.

"When I have kids, I'm going to raise them differently from the way my parents brought me up. Since I've calmed down a lot and no longer lose control, there won't be constant arguing in the

Donna, with her friend Marci: "*Now my highs come from the fantastic grades I've been getting in college.*"

house. In that respect, I've broken my family's chain. And I'm different from my parents in that I'm more aware of people's feelings.

"In two years I'll be graduating from college, which will be another first in my family. I want to become an elementary school teacher and also counsel drug and alcohol abusers. Mostly, though, I want to help children. If I can touch one kid's life that would make me feel great.

"People who knew me when I was on drugs and meet me now say I'm amazing. When they paint me as a superwoman or put me on a pedestal, I get uncomfortable. I wanted to quit drugs and that's why I stopped. I'm not doing anything that another person couldn't do."

AFTERWORD

TEN MONTHS LATER

ROB

Two months ago, Rob completed his treatment at the drug rehabilitation center. Before he graduated, he had to evaluate the program. "Absolutely pleased" were the words he chose.

While Rob no longer attends meetings at the center, he still goes there a lot to see his friends. Recently Rob has gone to AA meetings and plans to make that a once a month pattern. "AA forces me to remember what my life had been like," he says.

Right now Rob's taking a college literature course and is working toward getting a degree. "I'm not quite sure what I want to do yet, but whatever it is, I'll be good at it."

PAT

Pat has completed the one-year course he had enrolled in at the trade school, but because the construction and building industry is slow, for now he's working full-time as a mechanic's helper in an auto dealer's shop. He continues to go two nights a week for drug rehabilitation treatment.

Recently he moved out of his grandmother's house and got his own apartment. He celebrated Christmas with friends.

Pat's two sisters and his mother still live upstate, and Pat hasn't spoken to them for a while. "I'd like to help my sisters, but I know I can't. Instead, I'm trying to get Pat on course. That's what's most important to me now!"

KERRY

In the fall Kerry went back to her old public school and has made new friends there. She also has a boyfriend whom she's known for many years. He too had been on drugs and had been in rehabilitation counseling. On weekends, when they go to parties together, he urges Kerry not to drink. She tells him it's up to her to decide. For the past ninety days, Kerry has been clean—no alcohol and no pot relapses.

In school, Kerry has joined a drug and alcohol support group where ten people meet and talk about their problems. Once a week she goes to her therapist, and now and then she attends AA meetings. "I'm much more relaxed and calmer than I've ever been."

JOHN

John, who's been sober for two years and five months, goes to AA meetings four to five times a week. Besides his baby-sitting job and being a waiter, he takes two college courses, sculpting and acting. Last month he had a big part in a comedy. Now he's waiting to get accepted into college as a full-time student.

John says that for the first time he gets along with his stepfather. Through AA, they've learned how to talk to each other and forgive what's happened in the past. When they're together, they joke around a lot. "Dad trusts and respects me and treats me like a grown-up. Although I still can't tell him I love him, I definitely do—a lot."

DANIELLE

Danielle is doing well in her two-year college program and is now thinking of applying to a four-year school. Instead of becoming an accountant, she now thinks she'd like to be a teacher. That's what her boyfriend also plans to do.

She's told him about her past and in many ways he tries to help her. Instead of going to parties where there will be drinking, the two of them prefer the movies or other places where Danielle won't be tempted by alcohol. On their school vacation they went on a ski trip. Danielle says, "I'm so happy. I'm having a ball! I have no interest in that other life I used to lead."

JEFF

After being in the program for nine months, Jeff was dismissed by the drug treatment center. That means he could no longer have treatment there. To protect his privacy, the center would not tell why he had to leave. Their main reason for dismissing a patient is that the person refuses to respond to the treatment plan.

Jeff no longer lives with his parents. His family has not seen or heard from him since his treatment stopped. They hope that he is well and not hurting himself.

CINDY

Last month Cindy celebrated her fourth anniversary in sobriety. That night when she came to the AA meeting, cards and presents were waiting for her. "I was on a pink cloud," she says.

Recently Cindy got a new job where she types, files, works at the computer, and handles supply-ordering problems for a school system. With this more responsible position, Cindy's salary was raised. Still, she doesn't earn enough to pay for her private and group therapy, so on weekends she waits on tables and also cleans houses. Two to three nights a week Cindy goes to AA meetings.

"It's taken a lot of energy, but I'm finally able to make my own decisions without being afraid of making a mistake. Now I feel like a grown-up."

DONNA

Besides going to classes, Donna takes part in lots of school activities. She handles students' complaints in the education and psychology departments, and she headed the decorating committee for a recent dance. Because she baby-sits three times a week, she had to turn down other committees she would have liked to join.

Before the summer, Donna was in group therapy but now sees a private counselor again. Also, she has a boyfriend who works and who doesn't drink or do drugs. Like Donna, he enjoys sports.

Given a choice, Donna would love to spend the rest of her life helping people. "I want to get a Ph.D. in psychology and devote my time to keeping the sparkle in kids' eyes."

GLOSSARY

ACID: L.S.D.

ANGEL DUST: Powdered form of PCP (phencyclidine). Causes hallucinations. Unpredictable effects. Smoked in a joint, snorted, or swallowed.

BAD TRIP: Frightening experience after using hallucinogenic drug.

BAG: Small plastic bag measurement of marijuana or heroin.

BLACK BEAUTIES: "Speed." Stimulates the nervous system. Increases activity and alertness.

BLASTED: Extremely "high" or intoxicated state.

BLITZED: Slang for being high.

BOWL: Part of pipe that holds marijuana.

BURN OUT: Drug user who's high and intoxicated most of the time.

BURNED OUT: Wasted and washed-out feeling user has when coming down from a high.

BUZZED: To be high on alcohol, marijuana, or other drugs.

COCAINE: Stimulant that's inhaled or injected. Produces intense high followed by depression.

COKE: Slang for cocaine.

COLD TURKEY: Sudden withdrawal from drugs or alcohol.

CRACK: Highly addictive form of cocaine that's smoked in pipes. Produces intense but short-lived high.

DEALING: Selling drugs.

DIME BAG: Slang for $10 bag of marijuana.

DOWNERS: Slang for drugs that slow down or depress the central nervous system like tranquilizers or barbiturates.

FREAK OUT: Behavior of person who's had a bad trip.

FREE BASE: Changing the form of cocaine to make it smokable and more intense than when snorted.

GARBAGE HEAD: Person who uses any drug available to get high.

HIT: Single inhalation of marijuana or single dose of another drug.

JOINT: Slang for marijuana cigarette.

144

L.S.D.: Lysergic acid diethylamide. Also called acid. Extremely powerful. Causes hallucinations.

MARIJUANA: (Also called grass, pot, weed, hash). Drug from leaves and flowering tops of Indian hemp plant. Mostly smoked in rolled, thin cigarettes (joints) or in a pipe. Causes intoxication.

MESCALINE: From peyote cactus. Causes hallucination.

MUNCHIES: Extreme hunger after taking drugs, especially marijuana.

MUSHROOM: Psilocybin. ('shrooms, magic mushrooms). Produces hallucination.

OPIUM: From opium poppy. Added to tobacco or marijuana and smoked. Narcotic.

PARTY: Slang for getting high.

P.C.P.: Angel dust. Can be smoked in a joint, snorted, or swallowed. Causes hallucination.

PIPE: Used to smoke marijuana and other drugs like crack.

RELAPSE: Drinking or taking drugs again after withdrawal.

ROACH: Butt of marijuana cigarette that's been burned down too far to hold with the fingers. Instead it is held with a roach clip.

RUSH: Slang for instant high.

SNORT: To inhale powerful drugs.

SPEED: Slang for amphetamine or stimulant. Usually tablets (crystal meth, black beauties). Suppresses appetite, increases heart rate, and causes high energy level.

STONED: Intoxicated state, especially from marijuana.

STRAIGHT: Slang for getting off drugs and alcohol. Staying sober or "clean."

TRIP: Slang for experience caused by hallucinogenic drug.

WASTED: Slang for a high.

BIBLIOGRAPHY

FOR CHILDREN AND YOUNG ADULTS

Berger, Gilda. *Crack: The New Drug Epidemic*. New York, N.Y.: Franklin Watts, 1987.
Provides facts about crack, its addictiveness and dangers. Photographs.

Engel, Joel. *Addicted*. New York, N.Y.: Tom Doherty Associates, Inc., 1989.
Young adults in treatment tell their individual stories about their lives on drugs. Graphic language.

Hyde, Margaret O. *Mind Drugs*. New York, N.Y.: Dodd, Mead & Company, 1986.
Explains harmful effects of most commonly used drugs. Very informative and readable.

Mendelson, Jack, M.D., and Nancy Mello, Ph.D. *Cocaine: The New Epidemic*. New York, N.Y.: Chelsea House Publishers, 1986.
Offers history and other facts on cocaine use. Photographs.

Seixas, Judith S. *Living with a Parent Who Drinks Too Much*. New York, N.Y.: Greenwillow, 1979.
Provides anecdotes from children who live with an alcoholic parent. Author gives advice on how to cope.

FOR ADULTS

Barnes, Deborah M. "Breaking the Cycle of Addiction." *Science*, August 26, 1988: 1029–1030.
Describes various stages cocaine users go through as they try to break away from the drug.

Browne, David. *Crack and Cocaine*. New York, N.Y.: Gloucester Press, 1987.
Factual information about crack and cocaine and the effects these drugs have on the users.

Hurley, Dan. "Cycles of Craving." *Psychology Today*, July–August 1989: 54–60.
Details the new addictive drugs of the 1990's and what effects they have.

Le Vee, Joy. "Cocaine, An American Epidemic?" *Current Health*, November 1986: 3–9.
Describes effects of cocaine, the fastest-growing drug used among young people.

Inaba, Darryl S., and William E. Cohen. *Upper, Downers, All Arounders*. San Francisco, Calif.: Cinemed, Inc., WEC Films, 1990.
Details the effects of moderate doses of drugs on the average person. Describes various ways different drugs can be taken and the reaction the user might have.

Marriott, Michael. "Struggle and Hope from Ashes of Drugs." The *New York Times*, October 22, 1989, pages 1, 36.
Discusses what it feels like to be a drug addict.

Polson, Beth, and Miller, Newton, Ph.D. *Not My Kid*. New York, N.Y.: Arbor House, 1984.
    The author, parent of a drug-addicted child, gives readers an understanding of the drug problem to help themselves, their children, and their families get back to normal. Research included interviews with over three hundred children and their families.

Porterfield, Kay Marie. "Teen Drug Rehabilitation: The Inside Story." *Current Health*, February 1989: 19–21.
    Provides statistics and information on number of teens using drugs and how they respond to rehabilitation treatment.

Schwebel, Robert, Ph.D. *Saying No Is Not Enough*. New York, N.Y.: Newmarket Press, 1989.
    A book to help parents open discussion about drugs with their children to prevent the child's use of addictive substances.

Youcha, Geraldine, and Judith S. Seixas. *Drugs, Alcohol and Your Children*. New York, N.Y.: Crown Publishers, Inc. 1989.
    Presents an extensive list of "warning signs" of drug abuse. Gives examples of how parents should talk to their children about substance abuse, where to get help, and how parents can help themselves.

SOURCES OF HELP

Al-Anon/Alateen Family Group Headquarters
P.O. Box 862
Midtown Station
New York, N.Y. 10018
1-800-344-2666 (Including Alaska, Hawaii, Puerto Rico, and
Virgin Islands)
212-302-7240 (New York and Canada)
  24-hour answering service.

Cocaine Anonymous
See listing in area telephone directory.
  National self-help group to break addiction. Follows AA
12-step program.

Cocaine Helpline
1-800-Cocaine
  24-hour counseling service.

Family Anonymous
See listing in area telephone directory.
  For families of drug addicts—to learn how to take care of
themselves.

Narcotics Anonymous
See listing in area telephone directory.
  National self-help group to help break addiction by follow-
ing AA 12-Step program.

149

National Clearinghouse for Alcohol and Drug Information
P.O. Box 2345
Rockville, Md. 20852
301-468-2600
   Offers lists of treatment programs and information on alcohol and drug problems.

National Council on Alcoholism
12 West 21st Street
New York, N.Y. 10010
1-800-622-2255
(1-800-NCA-CALL)

National Directory of Drug Abuse and Alcohol Treatment and Prevention Programs
   Offers list of licensed treatment centers.
See listing in directory available in local libraries.

National Institute on Drug Abuse
1-800-662-HELP
   Information and referral on local treatment resources.

National Youth Crisis Hotline
1-800-HIT-HOME
   For intervention when there's a crisis at home.

Parent's Resource Institute for Drug Education (PRIDE)
1-800-241-9746

TOUGHLOVE
Parent support group.
1500 in the United States and Canada.
1-215-348-7090

INDEX

151

ABOUT THE AUTHOR

Maxine B. Rosenberg is the author of three previous books for Bradbury Press, *Not My Family: Sharing the Truth about Alcoholism, Growing Up Adopted,* and *Talking about Stepfamilies.* She is also the author of more than a half-dozen photo essays, including two ALA Notable Books, *My Friend Leslie* and *Being Adopted.* Her children's books spring from her experiences as a teacher and mother and from her personal interest in creating books that concern children's feelings. "I love interviewing children and listening to their stories," she says. "Even more, I love when children write or tell me my books make them feel more comfortable with their lives. Then I know I have chosen the right profession." Born in New York City, Ms. Rosenberg received her bachelor's and master's degrees from Hunter College. Now a full-time freelance writer, she lives in Briarcliff, New York, with her husband, Paul.

DATE			